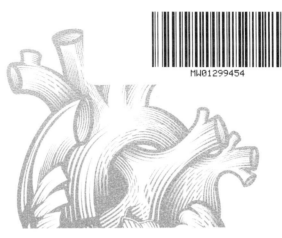

A Generous Heart

CHANGING THE WORLD THROUGH
FEMINIST PHILANTHROPY

KRISTEN CORNING BEDFORD

Contents

INTRODUCTION 3

PART ONE | Be Informed 15
Be informed about your passions, your resources, and the needs of your community
Chapter 1: You Are a Philanthropist 17
Chapter 2: Developing Your Values and Passions 31
Chapter 3: Establishing Your Resources 41
Chapter 4: What the Community Needs 49

PART TWO | Be Intentional 59
Be intentional with how you direct your resources
Chapter 5: How You Give / Strategies 61
Chapter 6: What You Give / Resources 79
Chapter 7: Creating Your Legacy 94

PART THREE | Be Joyful 109
Be joyful in giving and receiving
Chapter 8: Gratitude 111
Chapter 9: Simplicity 130
Chapter 10: The Map: Your Giving Plan 149

PART FOUR | Putting It All Together 153
Aligning privilege with purpose
Chapter 11: The Territory:
   Expanding the Limits of Your Generosity 155
Chapter 12: A Systems Perspective 169
Chapter 13: The Hive: Using Feminist Philanthropy
   to Change the World 174
Chapter 14: In Conclusion 182

Gratitude 188
Resources and Books 190
Works Cited 201
The Author 207

INTRODUCTION

In the early morning hours of an otherwise ordinary weekday, a shooting took place at a youth music venue in downtown Tacoma, Washington where I lived and worked. It was the first shooting like this that had happened in Tacoma for some time, and it was making headlines because it was in the heart of downtown and outside of a club which was operated by a well-known nonprofit organization. It also just so happened, in my role overseeing the grant program at the local Community Foundation, I had recently recommended funding for this new venture to provide teens with a place to gather and be creative, while receiving services that could help them get off the streets and away from gang violence. In the wake of the tragedy, I couldn't help but ask myself: had I encouraged support for something that wasn't viable, wasn't safe, wasn't in the best interest of the community?

When I got to work that morning, I sat in the boardroom with my boss, our CEO, under the still wet lettering of our newly adopted values, *Integrity, Leadership, Innovation, Collaboration*, to discuss our role and responsibility in the situation. I was questioning my due diligence and my complicity. Had I done the proper vetting? Could I confidently speak to the press, let alone our board of directors, about my recommended support of this organization? Was this music venue a benefit to our city or a magnet for troubled youth? Did I trust that the nonprofit was properly equipped to deal with these issues, and ensure the safety of their patrons and the wider community?

In retrospect I can see that I was asking the wrong questions. These are questions born of fear and power, of separateness and ego. These are questions asked by someone who bestows gifts from an ivory tower. And this was not the way I, or this foundation, wanted to operate. We were forging a new way of working with the community, and as our discussion continued that morning, I was reminded that the individuals running these programs were my trusted advisors. I valued their judgement and knowledge of the youth community they were working with, and I often relied on their expertise and leadership on youth issues. The path forward was clear: our "partnership" was meaningless if support was only offered when things were going well. In fact, partnership meant we should be there *especially* when problems arose. The CEO and I arranged a meeting with their staff and leadership, being clear upfront that their funding was not in jeopardy, to discuss their challenges and what we could do to further our support of their work.

The conversation that ensued was explicit and vulnerable. We discussed power dynamics and racial inequity and the challenges of working with a transient youth population in poverty and trauma. We laid our cards on the table: *this isn't just your problem, this is a community problem in which we are partners; this is about what we are going to do together.* In doing so, we made a commitment to construct a shared vision of addressing the youth violence we were both tackling with our varied resources, and took a small step toward solidarity. I could bring people to the table with political clout and financial resources, they could bring expertise and the youth voice. Collectively, we decided that the Community Foundation would convene a process with city leaders, other funders and youth that frequented the music club, with the intent to construct mutual goals around combating youth violence. It was a test of our desire to be a community convener, and the relationships and initiatives that came from this initial discussion changed the way a community engages with each other. It certainly changed me.

Our first gathering in that process stands out among all the other moments that came after. The adults were in business attire, accustomed to arriving to board room meetings. We were aware that these were young people with histories of gang involvement and school suspensions, which made us overly nice and contributed to the awkwardness in the room. The teens were confident but quiet, scanning the adults for intent. They had been selected to be part of this conversation because they were motivated to engage and strategize on how to decrease youth violence in our city—it was clear they understood the bias and discrimination they were walking into.

It was a pleasant afternoon, and the doors to the office stood open to let in a fresh breeze. To begin building relationships with each other, each of the adults paired off with a teen we'd never met before. I stepped onto the deck overlooking Pacific Avenue with a young boy, maybe 16, along with several other pairings of adults and youth. We were instructed to stand back-to-back with each other and start stating facts about ourselves, one at a time, until we hit upon a commonality.

Back and forth we went, stating where we were born, where our grandparents came from, our birth order, our favorite food, our favorite color, our eye color, what we wanted to be when we grew up, what our parents did for a living. Nothing about us lined up. I don't think either of us thought we'd get there. Then he said, "I've always wanted to travel to Japan. I want to learn Japanese." I whirled around, my eyes blazing, "Me too! Oh my gosh, me too!" We were chest to chest now, smiling at each other a ridiculous amount, like we'd just won a contest. Beyond all the categorical factors of our exteriors and experiences, there was a common dream, a shared humanity. We stood like this, laughing and talking about travel goals and why Japan held a special place for each of us, listening to the other pairs whoop with laughter when they hit upon something they held in common.

Now, I'm not going to say this connection changed the world. Or that there weren't still systemic power dynamics very much at play in that room. I certainly couldn't tell you whether this young man's version of the story was as impactful as mine. But what I can attest to, quite emphatically, is that it was the beginning of a bold experiment in community engagement. As we all came back together around the board room table, with those values hanging over our heads, our conversation deepened. The energy had shifted. The adults seemed lighter, as if we'd been reminded of who we were as individuals and why we were working with passion to make the world better in the first place. We were more authentic and vulnerable in our speech, noting that our titles didn't give us any more authority or agency in addressing the issues. In fact, it became clear that the experts in the room were those who had just finally been invited—the youth. In this space, the teens were emboldened to speak their truth and challenge our power. They were confident to question our intent and their ability to affect change. Together we recognized the opportunity to do things differently.

Toward the end of this meeting, one young woman pointed out that the working name of the group, Youth Violence Initiative, focused on the youth as being perpetrators of violence, rather than on the youth combating the violence. She suggested we reframe the conversation, calling ourselves the Youth *Against* Violence Initiative. She was, in fact, more direct than that when she stated, "You should let us lead." A collective silence filled the room for a moment, and there was no discussion needed: with

Youth Against Violence, those directly impacted would lead the conversation and the necessary change.

Due to this shift in power, a sustainable model of leadership was put in place, which understood reciprocity as a guiding principle. Recognizing and honoring our interdependence set the tone for all that we could accomplish. The Youth Against Violence community convenings culminated in young people being hired at the Community Foundation to help launch the first Youth Philanthropy Board. It also informed our strategy to support arts in the schools as a lever to keep kids in school, and it deepened our partnerships, from nonprofits to other funders and city leadership. This experience reframed my understanding of the potential of a Community Foundation, moving from a reactive grantmaker and fund holder for wealthy families to a dynamic community partner and strategic convener.

It was the beginning of a transformational process that created pathways of success for multitudes of individuals and community partners; and it validated my assumptions about power and privilege and the role of philanthropy in combating the most entrenched problems. I can recognize that it wasn't the beginning of my evolution, but it was a significant milestone. Through this process I experienced what it feels like to step authentically into relationship with others. And it set the tone for my future work as a philanthropist, to continually pose this question to myself: How do I embrace humility and enter a room not knowing the answers?

Most of my stories of growth come from listening to and following the voices of young people, even when I was still considered young myself. Bringing in those voices from the margins—those with the most to lose and the most to gain—has set me on my path to seek justice over charity and change the culture of philanthropy. Throughout my journey as a philanthropist, these individual encounters gave me a greater awareness and appreciation for the importance of diversity and equity in my work. It developed my framework of solidarity, reciprocity and agency in creating an informed, intentional and joyful giving practice—what I call 'feminist philanthropy'.

Writing this book has been instrumental in my journey as well. It's become apparent when I read back over it now, that the structure loosely follows my personal path, deepening into greater and greater awareness of the systemic issues at play in the world of 'giving' and 'doing good'. So while the beginning of the book starts out as a 101 primer on giving, it continues along a trajectory that comes closer to where my current thinking stands, a more political and activist approach to philanthropy. All of these rich layers of awareness, opening like a lotus across a pond of possibility, serve to strengthen my resolve to be better with each attempt. I hope by gathering these thoughts and putting them together in this way you will be inspired to deepen into your own philanthropy as well.

So in order to begin this journey, we need to create a shared understanding of what makes someone a philanthropist. *Who is this person?*

Just for a minute, think about a philanthropist. Someone you know, someone you've read about, or someone you conjure in your imagination. Close your eyes and flesh them out in your mind. Imagine what they are wearing, where they are sitting, what they are talking about. Imagine someone says to you, "Oh, you know so-and-so. *She's a philanthropist.*" What are your initial thoughts about this person?

You might be thinking of a specific person or you might have a general image not based on anyone in particular. Either way, it doesn't matter. Just establish a solid image of this person and take a second to consider the words you would use to describe them. Be honest.

I've spent a lot of time talking to people about philanthropy, and whether they are donors, volunteers, or recipients of nonprofit services, people equate the word and image of a philanthropist with great wealth and prestige. They use words like *rich*, *powerful*, and *strategic*. Someone once said "tweed pants." They mention Bill Gates and Oprah, or the giants of the industrial revolution, Andrew Carnegie and John Rockefeller. I hear about buildings named after men or wealthy white families, but sometimes, more recently now, someone will suggest a woman creating impact with her wealth.

When I push people to go further, I ask them to consider the qualities they admire in philanthropists. They might say "selflessness," "compassion," and "kindness." Sometimes they mention being inspired by their mothers or grandmothers because of their volunteering over a lifetime of giving. Yet they still have a hard time shaking the image of great wealth, and certainly feel uncomfortable using it as a description for themselves. The average person doing something good in their community doesn't consider herself a philanthropist—she'll refer to herself as a "donor" or "just a volunteer."

And yet, the amount of money you have, or give, does not determine your ability to be a philanthropist. The root of philanthropy is Greek, philanthropia, and it simply means, *to love people*. The dictionary definition of a philanthropist is *a person who seeks to promote the welfare of others*. Nancy Skinner Nordhoff is a thoughtful philanthropist whose giving supports women and the environment, mainly in and around her home on Whidbey Island in the Pacific Northwest. She made a comment about being a philanthropist that has become the basis of my work, and the impetus for this book. Nancy says, "I am not convinced that being a philanthropist is determined by the amount of money given, but by a generous heart giving as much as possible."

What I love about Nordhoff's definition of a generous heart giving as much as possible is how it allows for growth, flexibility, and learning. A generous heart is a muscle that can be strengthened, and giving "as much as possible" is personal and unique to each person at different stages in life. It opens the conversation to anyone who is ready and willing to make a difference. In this definition, those youth leaders at the Community Foundation are philanthropists as sure as any of the donors and board members.

Building on Nancy's definition of philanthropy, I've come to see that it takes three key attributes to be a philanthropist today (and it has nothing to do with the amount of wealth you have). A philanthropist is:

- informed about their passions, the needs of their community, and the resources they have to make a difference
- intentional about how they spend their resources
- and joyful in giving and receiving

In my work helping individuals identify what inspires their generous hearts, and how to create tangible impact with whatever resources they have, I witness the challenge of wanting to do good but being unsure of where to start. I began to construct a roadmap to support compassionate people in creating a life of philanthropy. In this roadmap I saw a desire to design a life better suited to support the needs of a whole community while being satisfied with having enough; I was intrigued by the concepts of minimalist living and right design and small living spaces; I was inspired by the ability of people the world over to live with hope, creativity, and kindness during unimaginable tragedy; I was energized by stories of generosity and the explosion of new ways of giving through social media. Through all of this, I was exploring how to be strategic with my own giving so that I could feel confident I was staying aligned with my values. I wrote this book out of a desire to engage with the idea of living in service to the greater whole.

True philanthropy is about social justice, design thinking, and storytelling. It concerns itself with relationship and engagement and ensuring a life well lived. This is true for the giver as well as the receiver. Philanthropy allows us to share what matters and why. It gives us a sense that the world, and our individual communities, can be better. Real philanthropy highlights how deeply we are all connected, to each other and the planet.

There is something new bubbling up through all of this. Whether creating sites that allow users to share their passions and increase financial support to specific issues or nonprofits, or using socially responsible investing to influence major corporations and governments, many people are working to connect the dots. We are witnessing a paradigm shift in the way we perceive the impact of our resources and how we view what our resources are. What most excites me is that this is an opportunity for each one of us to adjust our expectations of what we need in life and contribute something meaningful to our communities. This shift is providing us the prompt to develop a personal philanthropic plan that states what we care about in order to take action and live our legacies while we're still alive. We can witness the possibility of our collective impact when we align toward shared goals.

And this type of giving is uniquely feminist in nature. I am inspired by one of the central tenets of Fondo Centroamericano de Mujeres, a women's organization in Nicaragua, who write: "Feminist philanthropy is not a charitable act or an act of power. It is an act of solidarity and mutual empowerment." In this kind of philanthropy, your giving is a conscious political act. Here in the US, Charlotte Wagner, principal of the Wagner Foundation, and Catherine Gill, executive vice president at Root Capital are on the same page when they write "[feminist philanthropy is] about three things: collaboration, lack of ego, and intersectionality." Seeking creative, holistic solutions with courage and humility is the underlying ideology of the feminist movement as it works to create equality between the sexes and dismantle the patriarchy. The future of philanthropy hinges on equality across the political, economic, personal, and social spectrum, and using the lens of feminism can provide individuals with the tools they need to be more effective and innovative in their giving.

Feminism is not the belief that women are superior, or that men are bad, or that feminine things are bad. Feminism is a range of ideologies, and political and social movements that define, establish, and achieve equality of the sexes. Feminism challenges the system of patriarchy, which operates in conjunction with white supremacy. You do not have to be a woman to be a feminist or to practice feminist philanthropy.

This book is my contribution to the journey, encouraging others to visualize what's possible and get excited about their potential to heal the world. In the following pages, you'll find part inspiration and part workbook. I've included stories of people who have inspired me with their giving, and I've created opportunities for you to explore what your legacy might be and recognize what resources you have available to make a difference in the world.

In the first section, Be Informed, I lay out the ways to define what you're passionate about, what resources you have available to give, and how to figure out what your community needs. The second section, Be Intentional, walks through the basics of funding and lays out how to be strategic and smart with your giving. It also asks you to consider your legacy and explains how knowing this while you're still living greatly enhances your generosity. Be Joyful examines how a life of joyful giving and receiving is our greatest asset and will transform the world. In the final section, Putting It All Together, I ask you to explore the territory of generosity from a systems perspective in order to create a fully realized giving plan based on justice.

You might find that when you reclassify the giving you're already doing as a part of a larger philanthropic plan embedded in a personal legacy, your giving will expand. We all have something to give, and we could be doing a better job of it. By the end of this book I hope you will proudly declare yourself a feminist philanthropist, and encourage others to join you on the journey.

PART ONE | BE INFORMED

*"If people are informed they will do the right thing.
It's when they are not informed that they
become hostages to prejudice."*

—Charlayne Hunter-Gault

IN THE SPRING of 2014, a nine-year-old boy named Hector Montoya from Grand Prairie, Texas heard about a local fire that took the lives of a young mother and her daughter. Learning that some people didn't have smoke alarms in their homes, and the fact that a simple solution could have saved their lives, he decided to use the $300 he'd saved up to purchase a PlayStation 4 to buy one hundred smoke detectors for people in his community, and the local fire department installed them. He was quoted as saying, "... I decided saving a life was more important." Once Hector became informed about an issue, he acted on his belief that some things are more important than his immediate wants and needs. Hector is more than just a nice boy; he's a philanthropist.

Donors give money and volunteers give time; these are actions that are transactional in nature, they are things that you *do*. A philanthropist, however, is transformational. She recognizes that she is one part of a whole, and that her needs and wants are no greater or less than anyone else's. A philanthropist considers the larger implications of her actions, thinking strategically and acting with intention. She is motivated by a deep compassion and a sense of justice. The basis of philanthropy is unwavering love for others and an essential understanding of connection. It's time we embrace the word *philanthropist* to describe ourselves when we put others' needs before our own wants, because the words we use to describe ourselves send powerful messages about our values and our passions. What we call things matters.

Your journey in philanthropy begins when you seek information in order to understand your world and your role in it. First, you gain knowledge about yourself by discovering the story of your deepest passions and values. Then you tap into the breadth of resources you have at your disposal and discover creative ways to employ them. At this stage, the information itself becomes fodder for additional inquiry. Why you value something says a lot about where and how you grew up. How does this inform your giving practice? Recognizing the gifts you have to give says something about the value you place on your time and skills. How does this information expand or contract your ability to give? These are foundational pieces in your philanthropic plan.

Once you've created an informed internal compass, you can turn your attention to your community and your world. It's important here to also get a historical perspective on philanthropy, as this shines a light on the systems that make it necessary. Embedded in this knowledge is a maturing awareness of the part you play in upholding or challenging the issues and systems you're trying to influence and impact. Being informed means you can no longer look the other way when you witness injustice. You have developed curiosity and questioning, and you allow new information to alter your beliefs. Being informed gives you the stamina to commit to long-term action because you are no longer a hostage to unexamined prejudices.

CHAPTER ONE
You Are a Philanthropist

"One must be something in order to do something."

—Johann Wolfgang von Goethe

I HAVE a friend who is an accomplished artist, with gallery showings, commissions, and paintings sold—yet she told me that she hesitates to introduce herself to people as an artist. She feels the label carries ambiguity and expectation. *What does it mean to be an artist?* She compared these labels, artist and philanthropist, and I realized that the similarity is due to the fact that these words carry visions of actions that may or may not describe your skill or intent. More to the point, being an artist or a philanthropist is more about *who you are* than *what you do*. *Artist* and *philanthropist* are descriptive words that you recognize as integral to your character, regardless of how other people view you. You might be a well-known and revered artist, but being well-known and revered isn't what makes you an artist. Likewise, you aren't an artist just because you say you are, you have to back it up with action. You can't tell people you're an artist but never paint or write or sculpt, just as saying you're a philanthropist doesn't automatically make you compassionate and generous. You are something because you act on it, but how you act on it is part of the definition.

It's my mission to cultivate and nurture philanthropy in our communities, starting with individuals recognizing the power of their giving. Part of this conversation is rooted in understanding the enormous shift occurring in our economic system. There has never been a more important time to use everything you have to join the movement of doing good in the world. The needs are great and being a part of the solution is engaging and challenging and fun. My work in the nonprofit sector, both as a grant seeker and grant maker, had me mulling over this idea about increasing the pie. How do we find the means to support all the worthy causes in the world? How do we eradicate domestic violence *and* stop global warming? How do we address childhood obesity *and* keep animals from going extinct? It's not just about throwing more money at the problems, because often the problems get worse or they shapeshift into something else. We've gotten better at evaluating effectiveness and creating metrics to score charities doing the work, yet the problems persist. Sometimes we find we've been throwing money at the wrong things.

Philanthropy today is demanding we open ourselves to creating better systems: systems that understand money is just one element; systems that recognize that all people have value. Each one of us is a part of this solution, which makes it imperative that we develop an awareness of how we fit into the problem and a framework of how to talk about it. We need to understand the ways these problems are interconnected and acknowledge that each one of us is a node. Current technology is creating democratic ways of highlighting the problems and working together to solve them. But do each of us as individual nodes understand our responsibility and how to engage in the conversation? What could change if we knew we were philanthropists?

The next paradigm shift in creating change takes place on the individual level. Growing the pie isn't just about increasing the amount of money flowing into the system (there's already a lot of money in there), but about increasing the number of people who see themselves as philanthropists with multiple ways of giving. It's about restructuring the pie itself and questioning the roots of inequity. We need to recognize that we live within a construct that was only built a few hundred years ago and it is always evolving. We must create the necessary changes to make it work for the world we live in today.

The field of philanthropy has the potential to build a movement of people who align their resources with their values and passions.We need people who find a way to sustain their own focused giving to make small changes around them. And we also need people who reach around the globe to find the network of people doing the same thing. This movement is not limited to an elite group of people with extra money to give, or strictly about money for that matter. In *Give Smart*, Thomas J. Tierney and Joel L. Fleishman write:

> …the talent transfer is not even remotely confined to wealthy philanthropists. Teach for America is now the largest recruiter at several Ivy League colleges and major universities. In some cases it has attracted applications from over 10 percent of graduating seniors. Among older Americans, the appeal of encore careers is motivating those in their fifties, sixties, and seventies to engage in public service, through both volunteer and paid positions. People of every age are stepping forward to donate their scarce hours to communities and causes they care about—a far more precious and limited resource than any philanthropist's money.

The doors of philanthropy are opening wide and people from all stages and walks of life are streaming through. How each of us strategizes and creates a plan for giving will greatly enhance our ability to tackle the world's greatest challenges.

A brief history of US philanthropy

excerpted from Philanthropy New York

In the United States, philanthropy emerged among immigrants responding to each other's immediate needs. Strong religious beliefs promoted charity as a way to alleviate the problems of poverty. What we currently understand as modern philanthropy was built on industrial management methods popular in the business world at the end of the nineteenth century. The founding fathers of the philanthropy we're familiar with today—Carnegie, Rockefeller, and Ford—provided large-scale donations to address poor social conditions. In "The Gospel of Wealth," Carnegie asserts that personal wealth beyond what is required to meet the needs of your family should be regarded as a trust fund to benefit your community. Grassroots fundraising and volunteerism grew significantly during WWI due to nationwide organizations that still exist today like the Red Cross and United Way. These organizations helped to democratize charitable giving and volunteering, allowing individuals to contribute to causes in a systemized way. These efforts ultimately gave rise to the Community Foundation movement, which provided an alternative to national organizations, allowing regular community members of modest wealth to pool their money to create change at the local level which helped reshape small towns across the country. Additional legislation was passed in 1917 which allowed Americans to take tax deductions for their giving as a way to avoid personal income tax (a law that had been passed four years earlier). For the past one hundred years, philanthropy has remained largely unchanged: an activity for people of moderate or great wealth to help those lesser than them in exchange for tax breaks.

Paradigm Shift in Philanthropy

"You never change things by fighting the existing reality. To change something, build a new model that makes the existing model obsolete." —R. Buckminster Fuller

The rapid evolution of philanthropy over the last decade is due in part to the rise of technology and social networks, and the emergence of social entrepreneurship and social investing. And this technology is reminding us that philanthropy is meant to be democratic. Philanthropy is for everyone. We can all be strategic and thoughtful in how and when and why we give of ourselves. In the past, philanthropy was a straight transaction: you need, I give. The giving was often impersonal and contained a superior benevolence. In today's philanthropy, lots of people are involved, using various forms of resources, and they're working together on very personal issues. Feminist philanthropists are bringing relationships back into the equation, creating an interaction. This interaction, with all of us working together, is transformational; not only for those giving and receiving, but for the wider community they live in. This philanthropy looks different from the philanthropy of the past.

From Transactional...	...to Transformational
By the few; by the wealthy; by the older generation	By the many; by all income levels; by all ages
Donating money only; direct service aid; mostly local	Investing time, skills, ideas, money; systems approach; local and global
Through large organizations; give on your own	As a community; give with others; internet and phone apps
Broad humanitarian goals	Personalized projects with direct feedback

The emergence of social investing and civic engagement as philanthropic tools provides individuals with new ways to get directly involved with their giving. This transition shifts the power from the elite donor (a few individuals interested in direct service aid to broad humanitarian goals by donating large sums of money) to the network donor (many individuals of all income levels focused on using a systems approach and giving with others to personalized projects), and I would argue that we're quickly moving past the network donor to the hive philanthropist, someone with a feminist sensibility who operates as a whole and within a whole.

In addition, traditional charities are no longer the sole experts at solving social problems; social entrepreneurs have emerged with system-changing ideas. Technology and our ability to connect with each other as a global community has created opportunities for on-the-ground, real-time, tangible change with the click of a button. *Philanthropist* becomes synonymous with *changemaker*, and changemakers aren't satisfied with the status quo. Changemakers want to see the whole picture, shake up the systems within which we operate, and bring multiple stakeholders to the table. They want to get the job done.

Charity has been seen as something you do *for* and *to* others, while philanthropy can be understood as something you do *with* and *by* others. Similar to holistic health for a body, philanthropy addresses the underlying issues and grapples with the intricacies of unintended consequences, while charity is the medicine that takes away the pain for a moment.

For real change to occur there needs to be a one-two punch, artfully constructing a new reality by weaving charity throughout philanthropy. This employs a balance between using both your head and your heart. Philanthropy, unlike charity, has the ability to identify the interconnected problems and ascertain which are worth solving. A philanthropist today is aware of the levers of change and the ability of one person to impact a system. She recognizes the vast ecosystem in which we operate, and that there are many ways to shift power and possibility. Being an advocate for humanity and working to see the long view is essential to deepening your philanthropy.

We are at the nexus of change in how we understand our resources. We must acknowledge that while resources are finite, which forces us to be strategic and intentional, there are also numerous untapped resources still available to us (possibly just not yet understood or seen). I was listening to Neil deGrasse Tyson discuss the ways in which we perceive our world through our senses, illustrating all the currents of information around us that we don't tangibly feel, but which are very much real: radio waves, magnetic waves, light, and air currents. All this information is being transmitted around us, but most of it goes unperceived because we don't have the senses to pick it up. It got me thinking about all the resources we have available *to give*, both individually and collectively, that go unrecognized because it's not how we've been taught or expected to give…so we don't classify it as a resource. We actually don't *see* it.

Additionally, this idea of untapped resources shifts our accepted concept of "needy" to "grateful receiver" because it acknowledges that we all possess wealth of some sort. We begin to understand the dynamic nature of resources: we all have something to give. We're all in this together and in order to truly help people, you've got to get into the trenches and be with them. When we recognize our common story, our common humanity, we heave ourselves into the picture. No longer on the sidelines of history, we can now engage with the opportunity to participate in global change.

Building transformational change that is sustainable and actionable must always start with an understanding of the existing model and a deep personal commitment to seeing yourself in both the current and future vision. From the 2002 report *Transformational Philanthropy: An Exploration*, Duane Elgin and Elizabeth Share compiled nine components of transformational initiatives:

- Recognize that we have entered a time of global change and a historic window of opportunity
- Take a whole-systems, integral approach
- Build strength by actively embracing diversity
- Tell a bigger story about the nature and purpose of life
- Bring a reflective consciousness into the functioning of systems
- Foster self-organization at the grassroots level
- Provide leadership that ignites a belief in transformational change
- Approach change in transformational ways
- Recognize and appreciate multiple ways of knowing

If these bullets resonate with you, you're in the right place. Fighting against what already exists is a losing battle; we are being called to create a new reality.

Make It Personal

Hearing how other people discovered their passions is a helpful way to reflect over your own journey and tease out the threads that might make up your philanthropic giving. Below is my story of moving along a philanthropic spectrum, first getting exposure to an issue, then going deeper and making a personal connection, which ultimately led me to a greater understanding of my role and responsibility in creating change. Along with stories, we need tools, so I've included different approaches to become better informed about what you have to give and why, and what the community needs. This will be your foundation for the next section on giving with intention.

My Story

In 1998, to supplement my sporadic film production work, I picked up a few gigs as a substitute teacher at a private school. I had no idea how mesmerized I would be by the honesty and moxie of the girls in middle school. I had heard that girls at that age were horrible, self-absorbed, and emotional, but I was smitten. It seemed clear to me that they sat at the nexus of change for our society, that within their emerging womanhood they held the real solution to all of our problems. There was a light unfiltered, a story unfolding, that felt like a glimpse into possibility. Perhaps "horrible" was the dark side of this possibility when it's left unexpressed, muted, and ignored.

I didn't take this work at the school very seriously because I was in the film industry; it was a layover on my path to making movies. And yet, I felt a pull to do more than work in the entertainment world. So I started volunteering with Powerful Schools, a program that provides children who could benefit from additional adult influence with a "buddy" who comes to their school and spends one-on-one time with them. I was matched with a little girl in fourth grade, and I would spend an hour with her each week in the school library doing whatever she wanted. Sometimes we talked, sometimes we drew, sometimes we worked on homework. It wasn't a tutoring program specifically, though the kids selected by their teachers had challenging home lives and were falling behind or were having difficulty connecting with their peers. I can look back now and see the planting of a quiet seed of passion.

I met with her for two years in grade school and was encouraged by her teachers to stick with her through middle school. I was twenty-six and had absolutely no idea what her young life was like, but I knew I was getting as much from the relationship as I might have been giving to her. It took me years to realize what that was.

I remember a few instances vividly from my time spent with Maya. I remember when I presented her with a journal in fifth grade, with my phone number and email address, and told her that she could be anything she wanted. She looked at me shyly and said she'd like to be a doctor for babies. There was the day I showed up on the playground when she was in sixth grade, sporting newly bleached streaks of blond in my brown hair. As she came jogging around the track, she began to slow as she caught sight of me, then cut across the grass, hands on hips, shaking her head slowly back and forth. As she got closer I could see the downward turn of her lips, mouthing, "Horrible. Horrible." I laughed, and for the first time I saw her emerging as a young adult.

I think fondly of her graduation from eighth grade. She was hesitant the day she presented me with a ticket, asking if I'd like to come. I was the only person who attended the ceremony for her. I told her that middle school is really tough and she made it through. I told her I was happy to be in the audience celebrating her achievements and rooting her on into high school. I told her I was honored that she wanted me there and I wouldn't miss it. There's a picture of the two of us, silly beaming smiles, her holding the flowers I'd brought. It was the first time I met her mother, when I picked her up that night. I was incredibly nervous to meet the woman I'd only heard screaming on the other side of a phone, but found her to be sweet and thankful that I was driving her daughter that evening.

And I remember the day, four years later, when I showed up as her personal shopper at The Ruby Room, the nonprofit I'd cofounded to provide girls with prom dresses. She told me she was planning to attend summer school to finish up some credits and then start at a community college to pursue the interest she named when she was in fifth grade—to be a pediatrician. It was a capstone moment for me, to help her pick out her prom dress and hear about her plans for the future, nearly a decade after we'd first met.

It was also the last time I saw her, though we spoke and emailed for a while after that. I've never been able to locate her through social media, but I wonder sometimes when she'll show up in my life. This year she'll turn twenty-six, the age I was when I began meeting with her. Would I like her as an adult? Would she like me?

When I first met Maya she told me that her father loved her little brother more than her, and I assured her that couldn't possibly be true. It wasn't until our second year together that she informed me that her dad was in prison and the man she'd been telling me about for the past year was the father of her younger brother, and he didn't live with them. I also remember getting to school on several occasions to find that she wasn't there that day because her mom needed her at home to take care of her younger siblings. As I moved with her to middle school, the guidance counselor had to call Maya's mom to ensure she was still okay with me meeting with her daughter (the program I'd begun with didn't continue to middle school, so we were now meeting outside of the umbrella of a nonprofit organization), and I could hear the yelling through the receiver from the other side of the desk. I wasn't sure if she was upset at the counselor, or the idea of me, or just someone else in the house, but when he hung up the phone he just nodded at me and said, "Yeah, it's fine."

Women and Girls

This experience taught me a greater appreciation for mothers and how so many of them are working within a system rigged against them. My time spent with Maya gave me insight into a mother, and a family, in distress. I glimpsed the difficulties teachers have working with children when there are problems at home. And I understood that there are a number of interventions necessary beyond school and social services like "buddy" programs. I began to see "women's issues" in a new light: first as "family issues" and then further as "community issues." And I'm embarrassed to say, that it wasn't until many years later that I grasped how this was, at its core, a systems issue. These particular injustices are part and parcel of a system that is racist, sexist, and classist.

I developed a deep belief that the way to solve social problems was by supporting the young girl, who will become the mother. Give them opportunities for power and the tools to strengthen their voices so they are strong and clear, so that they can be at the frontline of addressing the systemic issues in their lives. When you put the girl in the center of the equation, you create sustainable solutions. While in graduate school in 2002, many years after I first started meeting with Maya, I read a passage in *Action Research: A Holographic Metaphor for Guiding Social Change* that said, "A hologram is a photograph, taken with a lens-less camera, where the whole is represented in all the parts. If the hologram is broken, any piece of it can be used to reconstruct the entire image. Everything is in everything else; just as if we are able to throw a pebble into a pond and see the whole pond and all the waves, ripples, and drops of water generated by the splash in each and every one of the drops of water thus produced…" This resonated with my belief that a girl's experience provides a mirror of our culture's desires and downfalls. And indeed, what might we learn if we used the two entities—the larger cultural self and the individual self of the girl—to reflect back to each other the present we are fulfilling and the future we are attempting to create. I think we can illuminate a broader perspective in which to view current culture by seeing girls as a holographic metaphor. By establishing a foundation for healthier women we would in turn be creating a healthier society, and vice versa.

As I transitioned into my role as a grant maker in 2004, I realized the power philanthropy held in this conversation. Using the lens of the individual and society to reflect each other provided a systems approach to giving. Specifically, I witnessed how philanthropy targeted to the needs of women could unlock many of the social problems we faced in our community. The nasty problems, the ones without an easy solution, the ones that are so inextricably linked to everything else that it seems like untangling a rat's nest of necklaces. Hunger, homelessness, child abuse…all of these things had a similar leverage point. Get to the young woman, provide an education, reproductive choices, engage her in a community that demonstrates her self-worth, and you'll see a ripple of change take hold in her family tree.

Studies continue to emerge showing that, more than changing her family tree, educating a woman and providing her with reproductive choices can also affect things like climate change. In Paul Hawken's book *Drawdown: The Most Comprehensive Plan Ever Proposed to Reverse Global Warming*, he writes that enhancing the rights of women and girls could improve the future of life on this planet. In fact, the education of women and girls is ranked #6 out of 100 solutions: "[E]ducating girls, as it turns out, has a dramatic bearing on global warming." Family planning is ranked #7, and these two strategies, working in tandem, have great potential for reversing and managing the impacts of climate change.

Focusing on women and girls as a strategy to improve communities and our planet has increasingly become common practice, but at the time when I was hanging out with Maya and going to grad school, I was feeling this revolution on a visceral level. As is so often the case, your tangible experience of something creates the fertile soil for knowledge to take root.

My work with young women, and one young woman in particular, became the spark that ignited my passion and deepened my relationship with the topic of women's issues. And over the years, I've come to realize that even this was merely an entry point to a greater possibility of a feminist philanthropy. It's not just about women giving, or about giving to women and girls. In fact, it's not necessarily about women at all—it's about bringing balance back to the power dynamic of giving and receiving. It's about championing the feminine across social, political, and economic sectors in order to change the world.

You become informed about the world by working with the places and people and ideas that you love, and you expand your love for those things as you become more informed about them. The studies that continue to emerge about the benefit of working with women to address our most pressing issues only serves to strengthen my commitment. But it's when I trace back through the years to where and when and whom I was willing to give great chunks of my time and attention (which are my most valuable resources) that I find my true generosity. I'm able to clearly see that nurturing and honing my passion drives my ability to give. If you aren't sure where your passions live, this is where we start.

CHAPTER TWO

Values and Passions: What Do You Care About?

"Find something more important than you are and dedicate your life to it."

—Daniel C. Dennett

Values

Passions start within your set of values. What you perceive has value in your world greatly determines what kind of change you want to see and how you will apply yourself to supporting that change. Often our values play out implicitly throughout our day, and it's powerful to make them explicit.

Below is a chart of values (feel free to add your own). Circle ten that resonate with you as important.

Adventure	Authenticity	Balance	Integrity	Wealth	Joy
Control	Peace	Power	Wisdom	Justice	Love
Faith	Recognition	Family	Creativity	Discipline	Education
Security	Friendship	Service	Forgiveness	Fun	Growth
Happiness	Status	Hope	Health	Spirituality	Humor
Success	Influence	Truth	Independence	Kindness	Progress
Self-reliance	Freedom	Humility	Generosity		

Now cross out five of them. When I run this exercise with groups of people, I hear a lot of groaning here. You can do it! Get focused.

Now cross out another two so that you have three core values to write into the box below. Yes, this is even more frustrating. *How can you go from ten to three values? All of these values are meaningful and you just can't possibly cut them down further.* The group goes into a full tailspin of whining. I'm not asking you to remove a leg. Often you'll find that one or two of the values fit neatly up and under the final values you chose. This is fair and legal in my universe. But reduce down to the three and list them in the box.

Your Values:

Look at your three words. Consider what they mean to you. How would you define them for yourself? Reflect on how they show up in your life and why they're important. How does each one support the other to create a three-dimensional portrait of what you're passionate about?

When I first did this exercise for myself I ended up with joy, integrity, and truth, and I wasn't entirely thrilled. I wondered how joy could be a *value*; it seemed too soft. And truth felt like a political statement, too hard. Integrity felt massive, too big for an individual to hold as a personal value. So my initial misgivings prompted me to explore how I define these words, as I encourage you to do. When I did this, and then put the three values together, I was able to see a complete picture of who I am. *Joy* carries the spirit of thanks and gratitude. *Integrity* is an alignment of words and thoughts with actions. *Truth* takes courage, to be your true self, to be authentic and live with intention. Put together, these values created the space in which I set my passions. I can look back at these three little words and recognize that understanding what they actually meant to me created the framework to establish my personal philanthropy. This was the beginning of my work creating the structure for the philanthroBE retreats for women philanthropists.

Passions

After creating the three-legged stool of values, let's move into establishing the issues you're passionate about. For this I've used an extremely comprehensive listing from WiserEarth, a web catalog of nonprofits created by Paul Hawken, which unfortunately no longer exists online. In all of my work, I found that this list, with the exhaustive compendium of subcategories, to be the most inclusive and helpful in giving a thorough and broad picture of the possibilities to engage in.

Go through this listing by first marking whatever jumps out at you. You won't be crossing any off, but after checking all the things that resonate with you, you can go back and rank them. This isn't an exercise to highlight all the issues that need support and that you know are important. You might be concerned about global warming, but do you get fired up when you read an article about refrigerant management and wind turbines? Some things are going to resonate more strongly than others, and if you pay attention, certain things will rise to the surface. And using the example from my story about Maya above, I realized that my passion for women and girls actually does have a direct link to global warming, which I'm also concerned about. But my entry into the conversation isn't going to be refrigerant management, it's going to be a girl's education. By staying true to what I love, I'm taking my place at the table with the resources I have available to give.

You might, rightly so, be concerned about lots of things, and you might be able to sense how they're all connected, but you are only as effective as your focus allows you to be. Being scattered is a surefire way to get nothing done well. You have a finite amount of time and resources and narrowing your focus and choosing an entry point is the only way to make a sustainable difference that will endure beyond you. These issues, your passions, might change and evolve as you go through life. Begin to engage deeply in one or two topics and you'll see that the conversation might take you in new directions. This is okay! And we'll talk more about how to artfully shift issue areas throughout your life in the next section. The important piece here, right now, is to get started on *something*. If you don't prioritize your giving, someone else will do it for you. Focusing puts you in the driver's seat.

What would you change if you had your way? What issues take priority for you when you think about the problems of the world? Begin by going through the list and checking all that resonate with you. Which ones jump off the page and make you want to learn more?

○ **Agriculture and Farming:** policy, water conservation and management, ecosystem management, gardening, soil conservation and management, organic farming, global livestock industry, rural farming communities, sustainable agriculture

○ **Air:** acid rain, air quality and pollution, indoor air quality, ozone layer

○ **Animals:** animal and plant trafficking, animal welfare and rights, endangered animal species protection, wildlife ecology, wildlife habitat conservation and management, wildlife law and policy

○ **Arts:** art and sculpture, arts activism, arts education, arts therapy, literature, performing arts

○ **Biodiversity:** biocultural diversity, biodiversity conservation, domesticated animal diversity, domesticated plant conservation, seed conservation

- Business and Economics: corporate ethics, ecological economics, ecotourism, environmental accounting, finance policies and institutions, green banking and insurance, microcredit, natural capitalism, responsible business practices, socially responsible investing

- Children and Youth: child and youth protection, child labor, children in armed conflict, children's health, juvenile justice, youth capacity building, youth education and empowerment, youth leadership, youth-led organizations

- Civil Society Organizations (Nonprofits, Philanthropy, Social Entrepreneurs): communication and mediation training, nonprofit law, organizational funding, organizational governance, organizational support and management, training for nonprofits

- Coastal and Marine Ecosystems: human impacts, invasive species, law and policy, pollution, ecology, coral reef conservation, mangrove conservation

- Community Development: community enterprise, community participation, community resources, community service/volunteering, dialogue and consensus-building, fundraising, leadership training

- Conservation: conservation area creation and protection, conservation biology, conservation policy, land restoration, land stewardship, natural heritage conservation, natural resource conservation, wilderness

- Cultural Heritage: cultural diversity, cultural heritage conservation, culture and sustainability, language revitalization, traditional culture, democracy and voting, democracy and civil society, democracy education, democratic reform, fair electoral process

- Ecology: evolutionary ecology, fire ecology, landscape ecology, microbial ecology, molecular ecology, mycology, pollination ecology, soil ecology

- Education: access to education, government and sustainability, environmental education, environmental resource center, green schools, literacy, natural resource education, public and government education, sustainability education

- Energy: alternative fuels, electric power, energy efficiency and conservation, energy flow in ecosystems, energy policy, energy security and sustainability, nuclear power, renewable energy, sustainable energy development

- **Fisheries:** aquaculture, aquarium trade, sustainable fishing, world marine fisheries

- **Food and Nourishment:** food aid, food literacy, food supply, global food supply and sustainability, hunger and food security, local food systems, malnutrition, diet, disease, and education

- **Forestry:** agroforestry, certified timber harvesting, forestry law and policy, global wood products industry, logging, plantations, sustainable forestry, urban forestry

- **Global Climate Change:** climate change, emissions trading, greenhouse gases

- **Globalization:** currency exchange, fair trade, globalization impacts, international debt, trade balance, transnational corporations

- **Governance:** global governance, good governance, government oversight and reform, institutional accountability

- **Greening of Industry:** consumption and green consumers, ecolabeling and certification, ecological footprint, environmental monitoring, industrial ecology, life cycle assessment, natural resource management, recycling and reuse, sustainable production

- **Health:** alternative medicine, asthma, cancer, ecological change and emerging diseases, endocrine disruptors, environmental health, environmental toxicology, green hospital movement, health care access, health education, HIV/AIDS, infectious diseases, malaria, medical biotechnology, pesticides, public health, sanitation, tuberculosis

- **Human Rights and Social Justice:** climate justice, disability equality, distributive and economic justice, environmental justice, ethnic equality, human rights and civil liberties, human rights and natural law, human rights education, human rights monitoring, human rights protection, human trafficking and slavery, rights and equality of LGBT, social justice education

- **Indigenous Peoples and Rights:** indigenous lands, indigenous peoples and cultures, indigenous rights

- **Inland Water Ecosystems:** inland aquatic ecosystems, lakes and ponds, riparian ecology and conservation, river-lake ecology and biodiversity, rivers and creeks, wetlands

- **Law, Policy, and Property Rights:** biological patents, conservation easements, crime and policing, environmental law and policy, international humanitarian law and war crimes, land reform, land tenure, land trusts and land conservation, land use policy, law and policy reform, legal services and representation, precautionary principle, prison reform and policy, property rights, restorative justice

○ **Media:** advertising, film, internet, journalism and the press, media and communication, photography, publishing, radio and audio, television, video

○ **Men:** male circumcision, men and violence, men's health

○ **Mining:** fossil fuels, minerals law and policy, mining and refining ores, mountaintop removal, sustainable minerals industry

○ **Peace, War, and Security:** arms trading, conflict resolution, land and naval mines, militarism and violence, military disarmament, nuclear disarmament, peace and peace building, protected areas, individuals, objects and property, weapons

○ **Plants:** endangered plant species protection, endemic plant species protection, ethnobotany, plant ecology

○ **Pollution:** chemical pollution, energy pollution, global pollution, hazardous solid waste, light and noise pollution, petroleum in the environment, pollution prevention and reduction, pollution remediation, toxic and hazardous substances, water pollution

○ **Population:** demographics, family planning, global migration, human population growth and impacts, refugees, internally displaced persons and migrants

○ **Poverty Eradication:** affordable housing, crises and disaster aid, poverty alleviation, squatter communities, sustainable livelihoods

○ **Religion, Ecology, and Sustainability:** ecopsychology, environmental ethics, religion and ecology, sustainability religious and spiritual issues, sustainable living

○ **Seniors:** senior volunteerism and mentoring, seniors' health, seniors' rights and participation

○ **Sustainable Cities:** ecovillages, infrastructure, sustainable communities, sustainable transportation, sustainable urban and regional planning, sustainable urban environmental services, sustainable urban power, transition towns, urban communications, urban ecology, urban revitalization, waste management

○ **Sustainable Design:** biomimicry, green roofs, sustainable building, sustainable materials

○ **Sustainable Development:** biological development, economic development, rural development, social development

○ **Systems Thinking:** whole systems change

○ **Technology:** appropriate technology, biotechnology, information and communication technology, sustainability and technology, technology transfer

○ **Terrestrial Ecosystems:** deserts and semideserts, forest ecology and conservation, grasslands and savannas, shrublands, sparse trees and parklands, temperate and boreal needleleaf forests, temperate broadleaf and mixed forests, tropical dry forests, tropical moist forests, tundra

○ **Water:** dams, groundwater, hydrology and the global water cycle, water and energy, water and sustainable development, water law and policy, water quality and health, water rights, water supply and conservation, watershed management

○ **Women:** female genital cutting, gender equality, trafficking of women, women and the environment, women's civic participation, women's economic development, women's education, women's empowerment, women's health, women's rights, women's safety from violence, women's vocational training

○ **Work:** employment, global labor, informal economy, living wages, vocational training, worker centers, worker health and safety, worker rights

○ Add your own:

Now that you've marked all the things that you're passionate about, go back and rank them. What are you *most* passionate about? You might think about what you're already doing, or find that what you're already doing doesn't rank as high for you anymore. Consider those places in your life that you give most of your energy, the things that get you excited and drive you to stay up late or wake up early. You might notice that some of these interests are specific to a problem you want to see solved or a specific place you want to positively impact. You will probably recognize that each passion has an angle, a unique subset of interest in that particular topic. Pay attention to the stories you tell yourself about each issue area. For example, under animals I marked down my love of elephants. It felt like an outlier when held up with all the other issues areas I marked as passions, but I realized my love for this animal was an arrow directing me toward my passion for the maternal, the bond between a mother and child. This drilling down allows me to further hone my giving.

This is where you can use your values as a filter to help narrow the list. When I narrowed my values to the final three (integrity, joy, and truth), I recognized that the ones I crossed out supported and helped define them. Under "integrity" is health and authenticity, under "joy" is humor and creativity, and under "truth" is education. Using these values as a filter over my nine issue areas of passion, paying attention to what each one means to me, I found that there was a good fit with some and a weaker fit with others. Joy, integrity, and truth aligned with women's issues, mothering, and education. They are values that also support what might be called "right design," aligning art and sustainable design for the benefit of humanity and the planet, similar to the concepts in the Noble Eightfold Path in Buddhism. Through this prism I can focus my resources and explore my community to see how what I have to give fits with what is needed in the world in these areas.

Write your top three passions down and think about how they might support each other. What are the common threads between them?

Your Passions:

Congratulations! You've put a stake in the sand to mark your interest areas. You've given yourself some parameters to work within and some direction of where to start exploring. When you focus your passion, you become a magnet for people and activities. You might find that opportunities appear to come out of the woodwork. Be open to new things and enjoy the adventure of exploring and talking with people. Let this begin a lifelong inquiry into what makes you tick and how your gifts are an expression of what the world needs. The two are one and the same.

CHAPTER THREE
Establishing Your Resources

WE ALL possess something to give. And whether it is money or time or attention, we are constantly in a state of giving. We often don't acknowledge the giving that we're doing as "gifts" or place them within a framework of philanthropy. Taking a hard look at all of the ways you are currently giving allows you to cultivate and nurture certain areas. After doing an inventory, you might decide you want a higher-paying job to provide more financial support to the causes you care about, or that you want a less stressful job so you have more time to give to your family. For the first time, you might view your networks or your interest in a certain hobby as viable sources of giving and include them in your philanthropic plan.

Consider the following examples in order to do a personal audit and make a comprehensive inventory of the things you have available to give.

Your time and attention:
- You allot your mornings to focused playing with your children.
- You make people laugh and put them at ease.
- You visit elderly residents at a retirement community and listen to their stories.

Your skills and strengths:
- You do the books for a low-income day care center.

- You offer pro bono website design for LGBT nonprofits.
- You enjoy fixing bikes for the neighborhood kids.

Your networks and influence:
- You instigate and inspire others to come together.
- You know people with untapped resources.
- You have a wide social network and influence on social media.

Your money:
- You start a giving circle in your community.
- You build a "giving back" philosophy into your business plan.
- You pledge your friend to support her in a charity run.

Your stuff:
- You have a garage full of sports equipment that you don't use anymore.
- You've collected an assortment of designer purses that sits in your closet.
- You have multiple sets of china that have been passed down to you.

Taking stock of the resources you have available is essential in deciding what portion you'd like to give away. This takes some time to evaluate, but it's pivotal in creating a comprehensive giving plan. This is an interesting exercise because it can highlight where you have room to grow. You might be surprised to find there are opportunities for giving you weren't considering.

I'm an advocate for being insanely creative with what you have available to give, because at the heart of philanthropy *is our desire to give away our life energy to make something better.* Think about that for a minute. You are exchanging bits of yourself to create something outside of yourself. This is the totality of what life is: an exchange of energy and resources. Just as we breathe in and out, exchanging oxygen and carbon dioxide with the plants and animals around us, we are in a dance of giving and receiving with everything on this planet. How you spend your life energy is the topic of Section Two, where I'll go into much more detail. But for now, just consider that everything that comes from you is a gift to the world (or a curse as the case might be). You have the potential to give as much as anyone else, depending on how you structure your giving.

What resources do you have to give in each of these categories?

○ Time and Attention
○ Money
○ Skills and Strengths
○ Stuff
○ Networks and Influence

An important component of clearly seeing what you have available to give is acknowledging that you can't give what you don't have. It's easy to see when we use the china as an example. You wouldn't say to someone, "Oh, I'll give you this china set to sell and we can use the money to buy supplies for the hurricane victims" if you don't have a china set sitting in your closet. Yet we consistently do this with our time and money. We overcommit our days, and we spend on credit. If we begin viewing our intangibles as realistically as our tangibles we'd be able to develop a much clearer view of what we have available. It's worth repeating: *you cannot give what you don't have.* If you don't have networks or the patience to provide your full attention, you can't give these things. You might decide to cultivate them by spending more time nurturing personal networks or finding ways to take care of yourself in order to have more patience. A philanthropist looks squarely at what she has, recognizing the layers of resources lying around in her life, and makes a commitment to take care of herself in order to take care of others.

There was a retreat participant one year who was coming through a divorce and dealing with lots of expenses and emotional exhaustion. She worked full-time and was an engaged parent of two young boys. She was adamant that she didn't have anything to give, no extra money, no extra time. But as she talked with us about playing volleyball, which was her personal passion and the way she nurtured herself, she told us that a light bulb went on. She was heavily involved in creating and maintaining the sand volleyball courts in her town. She wasn't paid to do it and it was done in her free time. She had never recognized that activity as volunteering or philanthropy because she enjoyed doing it. The group had a good laugh as we realized how often we don't count the things we enjoy doing as philanthropy because somehow we've developed the notion that giving of ourselves should be a sacrifice.

We think of philanthropy as this activity outside of ourselves, somehow separate from our day-to-day lives. Yet philanthropy is an act of love that comes from a place of our deepest passion. If we maintain the stance that it starts with you being generous with yourself, then it should definitely feel good. If giving of yourself feels bad you need to revisit how and why you're giving. You might be giving from a place of depletion or to an organization or activity you no longer believe in. You might be giving from a misplaced sense of obligation. I strongly believe this kind of giving does more damage than it does good. The intention and emotion behind a gift carries energy. Commit to only putting out the very best of yourself and being intentional with how you share your life energy.

There's a great example of this concept shared by Lynne Twist about her early days of fundraising. Lynne is a teacher, writer, and consultant whose book, *The Soul of Money: Transforming Your Relationship with Money and Life*, greatly impacted me when I first started in the philanthropic field in my twenties. She is the founder of the Pachamama Alliance, an organization "which empowers indigenous people of the Amazon rainforest to preserve their lands and culture while educating and inspiring individuals everywhere to bring forth a thriving, just and sustainable world."

Lynne tells a story at the end of her book about traveling to make two very different "asks" to raise money for the nonprofit she was working for at the time. She meets the first donor, a male CEO, in an opulent high-rise in the Midwest, and she's nervous sitting across from him. After making the pitch for financial support, the man hands her a check that he'd already written before her arrival. It is the largest individual gift she'd ever raised, and while she is gracious, she's also aware that the CEO is giving this money to rectify the company's poor reputation. It's not a gift being made because he's been moved by her pitch or the needs of her organization.

She catches a flight for her next donor meeting, which is in a church basement in Harlem. She notices there are pans scattered around the room to catch the rain that's coming into the building. So again she's feeling nervous, but this time because it feels uncomfortable to ask people for money who seemingly are in need of it themselves. There's a long, uncomfortable silence after her pitch until finally a woman stands and introduces herself. Gertrude says that she doesn't have a checking account, and she only made $75 that week. But because she likes Lynne and her presentation, she's going to give some money. Each person in the room follows Gertrude's lead and comes up to give Lynne a donation.

Right away Lynne is affected by the responses from two very different donors. Back at her hotel, she considers the difference in intention behind each of these meetings. Gertrude's gift is an act of deep and personal generosity and it leaves Lynne feeling uplifted and hopeful. The CEO's gift carries a weight that made Lynne uncomfortable. After thinking it over, she writes a thank-you note to the CEO encouraging him to donate to something that speaks to his heart and she sends the money back. *Can you even imagine?* I'm not sure how you'd go back to your organization and explain this decision to a board of directors. But Lynne is compelled to stay in alignment with her values and the organization's mission. Many years later her decision is validated when the (now former) CEO of the company reaches out to tell Lynne that he was deeply impacted by her note and after a lot of reflection, he decided to send a personal gift five times the amount of the original donation. An amazing return on what was, at first blush, a really ridiculous thing to do as a fundraiser.

This same scenario happened recently in my hometown, when a donor sent a large gift to the Girl Scouts of Western Washington with the caveat that it was not to be used to support transgender girls. The gift represented nearly a quarter of the council's annual fundraising goal, but it went against the core values of the organization. It was a challenging decision, but not a difficult one. Megan Ferland, the council's CEO, stuck close to the organization's guiding principles and decided to return the gift, honoring the Girl Scouts' mission to serve "every girl." Ferland then launched an Indiegogo campaign asking people to help raise the $100,000 donation they had to return. And, similar to Lynne's experience, by respecting the power of staying aligned with purpose they raised over $185,000 *in just one day*.

These stories beautifully and meaningfully illustrate how giving money is a way to channel energy, which can be either positive or negative. Money is a powerful conveyer of story, and gifts like this are two-way streets, needing both the giver and the receiver in order to make an impact. The gifts from the first donors, whether as guilt money or money attached to strings, are business as usual. Questioning this relationship, staying true to mission and aligned with values, will ultimately resonate with the right people. And sometimes this means you need to meet the wrong people first.

My favorite part of Lynne's experience is the implication of impact. Lynne makes the clear point that she is not the one responsible for the CEO's shift in thinking. Gertrude's selfless act of generosity shifted Lynne's perception of giving, which in turn had an impact on the CEO. This gift, minimal by fundraising standards but *one that was as much as was possible for Gertrude*, inspired change in the minds and hearts of other philanthropists that unlocked even greater potential and greater generosity. It's a story that has many layers, from giving from the heart to knowing that your intention has the possibility of impact out beyond your sightline...and this story of Gertrude continues to be told to new audiences over and over.

Yet it wasn't just the gift that was given that created change. It was that the gift was given to the right person (who had the gift of magnifying it and sending the message out broadly) at the right time (when the distinction between a gift of intention was clearly outlined next to one of guilt). Gertrude understood her resources and came to Lynne's presentation passionate about the issue, aware of her ability to give, and prepared to do so.

This highlights the wu-wei of informed philanthropists. Wu-wei ("ooo-way") is a Chinese concept of "no trying" or "no doing," a state of mind that allows someone to be fully present, aligned with their actions so that effort flows from them effortlessly. They are in rhythm with themselves and everything around them at the same time, adjusting and reacting appropriately, as natural as breathing in and out. This is what well-known Hungarian psychologist Mihaly Csikszentmihalyi described as "flow" or *being in the zone*. When you are experiencing wu-wei as a philanthropist, you know your passions and resources and are prepared to act effortlessly and spontaneously when the time is just right. Gertrude was in the flow, secure in her ability to give and, finding herself in the right place at the right time, able to maximize her small gift by the circumstances around her.

Establishing your resources creates clear boundaries about what you actually have to give and begins to build your giving plan. Just as you might reach for either a broom or a hammer depending on the household job, peering into your philanthropic toolkit you'll know what you have available in order to accomplish a certain giving goal.

CHAPTER FOUR
What the Community Needs

BEING INFORMED isn't only about knowing what you're passionate about and what you have to give. The point of philanthropy is that it is tilted outward, focusing on how you contribute back to the world you live in. With your passions established and your interests narrowed to three topics, you can now spend time researching and learning about the landscape of these areas of interest. Discovering what the community needs starts by engaging with and listening to people in the community, testing and validating your assumptions in order to create purposeful action. All the while you remain ready to recalibrate with added insight in order to continue tackling the issue with new perspective.

This circular process of learning elevates philanthropic work to that of changemaker. Part of this cycle of learning, reflecting, and doing is embedded in the personal journey too. You uncover prejudices you didn't know you had and recognize privileges you might not have formerly been aware of. These are the philanthropists our world is in need of—curious and engaged, ready to change course as new information comes in. Above all, valuing knowledge and an understanding of how the world works, and how it could work better.

In the United States alone there are currently over 1.5 million nonprofits, and this number doesn't include the ones who aren't required to file a 990 with the IRS because their budgets are less than $25,000 (Foundation Center). Throughout the entire world there are many more nongovernmental organizations (NGOs), easily twice what gets reported in the States. This is where being informed about what you want to do and how you want to give will pay off. Doing a targeted search for types of programs, projects, or people you want to support will make it more likely you'll find a cause that you can get behind for the long term. Directories like Guidestar and Charity Navigator provide general and financial information as well as evaluations of effectiveness and are essential tools to help make informed decisions about where to donate. Giving Compass is a comprehensive website that provides articles, research, and videos detailing specific issue areas as well as ways to connect through events, seminars, and webinars to lead philanthropists to more informed and strategic giving strategies.

Locally, your community foundation is usually a great place to start, as most have online catalogs of vetted nonprofits in your immediate area. But they, like the websites listed above, usually won't capture the really small organizations, the ones without the social capital and financial ability to even apply for foundation grants. And depending on the size of your community foundation, they might not be able or willing to take your specific phone call inquiry. I worked at a midsize community foundation in a smaller city and I loved the opportunity to meet someone for coffee who was interested in better understanding the community and how they could make an impact. I considered it part of my job to be on the ground listening to individuals regardless of financial ability, as it offered me insight into what the community needed and how I could help direct grants and connect donors. Because I believed the power dynamic between funder and grantee could get in the way of important work, and because I knew enough to know how much I had to learn about my community, it felt like an imperative to meet with people face-to-face when they asked. While most foundations will do this legwork for their clients who hold donor advised funds, they don't have the capacity to meet with just anyone as I did. However, many community foundations support special interest funds and donor circles who are made up of community volunteers, and if you are passionate and know something about an area they fund, you could be a great asset to them. To find a community foundation in your area, the Council on Foundations provides an interactive map.

Having access to so much information and the great needs in our world can be overwhelming, and when people get overwhelmed they shut down. This is why I encourage people to consider small acts of kindness and community service a part of their philanthropy. Again, this is the balance between looking out to the horizon and being aware of the larger systems at play, while having a softer gaze that's closer to home. You can start with yourself and recognize some of the small differences you can make in your community. From attending a school board meeting or asking a local business owner about their current challenges, to planting a garden or starting a meditation practice, actively engaging with the world, even through the subtlest activities, will take you in new directions that might lead to creative connections and collaborations to further your vision and develop your passions. The pivotal component is educating yourself to better understand the what, where, why, and how of an issue.

And don't underestimate the power of conversation with the people in your life. So often when we meet people we ask, "What do you do?" when a more interesting conversation might come out of asking, "What issues are you passionate about?" and "What did you learn today?" You might be surprised to learn that your great aunt Mary has given to Planned Parenthood for the last twenty-five years and will share the personal story of why she's been a longtime advocate, or that the mom who is running late to pick up after school on Wednesday is coming from a board meeting for the local food bank and would love to talk with you about the needs in your community. People have stories to tell, and unless we ask the right questions we miss opportunities for meaningful conversations that elevate us out of our day-to-day routines. Asking new kinds of questions is a practice that is imperative when informing yourself about what the community needs.

Asking the Right Questions

The right questions have the ability to instigate innovation and creativity. They lead to movement and ownership. They create change. Most of us were taught that questions have right and wrong answers; we were not taught how to formulate questions that elicit change. In Fran Peavey's strategic questioning model, she outlines the case for the strategic question:

> What would our world be like if every time we were listening to a gripe session, someone would ask, "I wonder what we can do to change that situation?" and then listened carefully for the answers to emerge and helped that group to begin to work for change? What would it be like for you to do that in your work, family or social context? Your attention and context might shift from a passive to an active one. You could become a creator, rather than a receiver, of solutions. This shift in perspective is one of the key things that people need in our world just now. And the skill of asking strategic questions is a powerful contribution to making such a shift.

And shaping a strategic question is indeed a skill. It's the most important part of understanding a problem. Einstein understood this when he purportedly stated, "If I had an hour to save the world, I'd spend the first fifty-five minutes understanding the problem, and the last five solving it." To solve any of the world's problems, we need to inform ourselves by asking open-ended, strategic questions. This level of understanding introduces you to the players involved and gives you perspective, on both the issue and your role in it. Peavey defines a strategic question as:

- Creating knowledge by synthesizing new information from that which is already known.
- Awakening the suppressed possibilities of change embedded in each person, in each institution, and in each society.
- Empowering ownership of the new information so the ownership of the information stays with the person answering the question.
- Releasing the blocks to change and new ideas.
- Facilitating people's own responses to change.
- Generating energy to make changes happen.
- Creating answers that may not be immediately known but may emerge over time.

The right question is the basis of good design thinking—the kind of thinking that takes us to a new level of understanding. It's the kind of thinking that allows us to suspend our judgments and consider alternatives. Good questions tap into our curiosity, get to the root of something, create bridges to other ideas and people, and ultimately pull back the curtain of our status quo. These questions push us to examine our role in the injustice we're trying to solve; without this kind of inquiry, when we shy away from the tough questions, we can stay safe inside our bubble of perception. When considering getting involved with an initiative in your community, you might ask yourself:

- Are the people directly affected by this issue considered experts in addressing the problem? Are they included in the conversation? Are outside experts working with those impacted by the change?
- Is this a grassroots issue, and if so, is it being handled by a local or national organization? (One is not necessarily better than the other, but again, pay attention to who is holding decision-making power and what voices are at the table.)
- Are there strategies that seem to be working, here or elsewhere? Successful strategies might come from other fields of work, from nature, from children playing at the park.
- How are my actions contributing to this problem? What actions might I take personally to alleviate this problem?

If you don't know the answers or can't find the answers, it might be because you need to get personally involved. This might mean, as a first step, doing your own reflection work and reading more about the topic. Some of these questions help expand your thinking about the issue, giving you pause to wonder about the scenarios that people find themselves in. Questions that start with *I wonder why…?* and *I wonder if…?* are meant to challenge your ideas of need; to seed a conversation with yourself about how *what* you believe about the issues influences *how* you interact with the issues. Understanding an issue, both from your perspective and from the perspective of those affected, makes it personal so that you can speak with conviction and care deeply about how your involvement makes a difference.

Reframing questions from ones that search for tangible, immediate answers into ones that get to the desire of what is being accomplished leads us to better understand the roadblocks. For example, rather than asking "How can we provide more housing to protect women escaping domestic violence?" we could start by asking "What do women need to be safe from abusive partners?" People will respond with the basics: "They need attorneys to represent them, they need to know that their children are safe, they need a car, they need a support system, they need job training, and yes, they need housing." But if pushed, what is the real, true answer to "What do women need to be safe from abusive partners?" The answer is: Women need partners who do not abuse them. Now that gets us into a completely different conversation. As a society, how do we support families, men and women, from being abused? What do we value about a healthy family? How do we teach our young boys what is acceptable? What systems are in place to support the emotional and mental stress on men in our society?

It should go without saying that, of course, women fleeing domestic violence need immediate support in the form of all the things mentioned above. However, if we are searching for systemic leverage points—the places to intervene in order to stop the cycle of abuse—we'll never get there by asking closed and directed questions. The real problem is a lack of imagination. The ability to step back and say, "What if?" What would the world look like if women were not being abused? What systems and resources need to be in place to facilitate this world?

It takes courage to ask the strategic questions. Some people might think you're being flip when drilling down to this level. It can come across as cruel or inadequate to push for a broader question and not deal with the immediate fire that needs to be put out. I like to take the naïve stance, the one that is curious about the seemingly impossible. We live in a world full of assumptions and unquestioned privilege that many of us take for granted. Probing for the story underneath the status quo is what allows us to course correct and build a better system.

And if your questions are met with simple and immediate answers, they probably weren't big enough questions. Find a question that haunts you, that leads you into new territory and won't let go. Where is the intersection between your passion and what the world needs? How might you be the person to fill the gap? As John E. Kelly III, IBM's executive vice president, said, "In the 21st century, knowing all the answers won't distinguish someone's intelligence—rather, the ability to ask all the right questions will be the mark of true genius."

With everything we've covered so far, you're becoming an informed citizen, an active participant in the needs around you. You've solidified the issues you're passionate about and what you have available to give, and you've got a handle on what your community might need from you. Now it's time to look deeply at how to align these things with your intention. How do you make the most of your resources? How do you know your giving is making a difference? What does success look like, and when will you know that you've achieved something with your giving? Philanthropists with assets big and small are asking these questions to better validate their giving and ensure that they're supporting sustainable change. The rub is, of course, that once you tweak the system, it's going to create unintended consequences. In addition, we all know that some things in life simply cannot be measured for appropriate outcomes. Being intentional is my answer to walking into the conversation with integrity and the long view.

PART TWO | BE INTENTIONAL

"The more you know, the less you need."

—Aboriginal Proverb

Being intentional with your giving is simply being thoughtful and authentic in your actions. It's aligning what you say with what you do, putting mindfulness into action. Intentionality is a way of slowing down, paying attention, and being precise in how you move through your life. With study and practice it becomes an integrated core component to your day-to-day living, developing self-awareness and a steadfast plan of action. Giving with intention makes your gifts an extension of your most authentic self, an expression of the heart.

The heart swells when it is aligned with its purpose and feels that its passions are being served. In other words, we can't all give away millions of dollars or create a social network that creates systemic change, but we can use what we have to do what we can. All of the elements you highlighted in the previous chapter—your time and your money, your networks and skills and stuff—all of these things make up what you have to offer to the world. These are your resources. This is everything you have available to give. How you spend these resources reflects deeply held beliefs about money and wealth, and about your legacy and what you care about. When you become clear about how these things move into and out of your life you create intentionality.

And when you tie these seemingly small acts into a strategic plan of action they take on a much bigger life.

In this section you'll develop a personalized guide for your philanthropy by contemplating your legacy and creating a thoughtful giving strategy. We start by going into the specifics of how to support nonprofits in a very traditional sense, touching lightly on topics like capacity building and exit strategies. These are key considerations when you're taking those elements of passion you uncovered in Section One and creating a philanthropic plan. Having a basic understanding of the classic donor issues, and being informed about what nonprofits will expect, allows you to get creative and explore new ways of giving (like social investing and creating neighborhood cohesion), but only after you've developed a personal toolkit from which to operate. These things create a framework, and throughout this section we'll work our way backward into a clear legacy that you can confidently drape across the structure.

With intention, your giving becomes a beacon for others to join as well. As you streamline your giving, attention is focused on the issues that matter most. All the inconsequential things that clutter our days fall away, leaving only powerful stories and opportunities for connection and change.

CHAPTER FIVE
How You Give

THERE ARE as many ways to give as there are things to give away. Figuring out how you want to give can be a complicated, formulaic challenge. Or it can be a simple logic model: if this/then that. There are many levers of change and a lot of ways to get involved, from addressing immediate needs to creating systemic solutions. You might start with one or the other and change course as your life changes. Intentional philanthropy isn't stagnant. It's meant to evolve with you.

My current evolution in philanthropy is leading me to reconsider immediate needs over my preferred systems change work. This is due, in part, to developing a family giving plan that involves my young sons. At their age it's much easier to include them in the type of giving they can see and feel. Learning about immediate needs in a community is the first step toward understanding the broader systemic implications of the complex problems we face. So I'm certain as we learn together, as a family, about the building blocks of need, we will someday return to tackling system-wide issues when the boys are older. Intentional philanthropy reflects your most genuine self, at whatever stage or situation you find yourself in right now.

Intervening in a System

Where do you intervene in a system to make the most impact? There are philosophical implications to each end of the giving spectrum, and where you give is as much an indicator of where you are in your own life, as it is a sign of how informed you are about a system. There was an episode of *No Reservations*, a show that followed chef Anthony Bourdain around the world on culinary adventures, that illustrated the challenge of helping people, regardless of where you intervene. It was as tough an episode to watch, filmed in post-hurricane Haiti, as it seemed to be to film. There is a pivotal moment when Anthony decides to buy all the remaining food from a woman cooking on the street and give it to the kids standing around watching them film, kids who haven't eaten in days. And what happens?

As the observer you can see it coming. Long queues form, someone uses a leather belt to whip back the crowds, and, as Anthony says, "It all turned to shit." You get that knot in your stomach that tells you that your "help" did nothing but make you feel good about yourself for a moment and relieve a temporary pain for others. Your "help" created unintended consequences. The difference I see between charity and philanthropy is illustrated beautifully in this moment in Haiti: charity helps by doing *for and to others* while philanthropy helps by doing *with and by others*. What this means, essentially, is when you want help people, you've gotta get down in the trenches and be with them (it's interesting to watch Sean Penn in this episode showing how this is done).

Anthony muses on the fact that the problem was thinking with his heart rather than his head, but in these situations it's imperative to do both. This is where working *with* those you're serving is key. If Anthony had asked the woman serving the food how best to distribute it, I bet she would have had some good ideas. Or maybe he could have selected some of the kids sitting at the table with him to work with the crew for the week in exchange for meals. It's an impossible situation, one that people the world over are trying to solve. How do you meet the immediate needs while building and sustaining a way for people to move beyond immediate needs? It's a balance between serving with your head and your heart, working logically with compassion.

Your personal philanthropy might be based on emotional connections, and giving to immediate needs doesn't mean you're not a philanthropist; however, giving without being informed about how and what and why you're giving will not be as effective. And without being aware that there will always be unintended consequences, you are not prepared to address the very real consequences of your intervention. This kind of giving is more self-serving than changemaking.

Consider the following four levels of intervention, adapted from Tracy Gary's book, *Inspired Philanthropy*, which illustrate the spectrum of philanthropy from transactional, *doing for and to*, to transformational, *doing with and by*. On the one hand, providing immediate care in emergencies, from food and clothing to housing and medicine, can satisfy donors looking for a firm grasp on where and how their time and money is making a difference. This can be personally rewarding giving, and in emergencies it is absolutely critical to ease the immediate suffering and trauma. But it also might barely scratch the surface of the needs at play. On the other hand, focusing on system-wide change tackles the deeply entrenched inequality and injustices in our established systems, looking for reform and shifts in consciousness, but it won't necessarily help the hungry woman standing in front of you. System-wide change is laborious and many donors lose interest due to the length of time necessary to achieve anything tangible. In between these extremes are levels of personal and community empowerment, which build infrastructure and personal responsibility.

Four Levels of Intervention

- **Needs:** focuses on urgent, critical needs; the tip of the iceberg; reactive
- **Empowerment:** builds individual assets and encourages self sufficiency
- **Capacity Building:** fosters collaboration and expands leadership in the community
- **Systemic:** deals with root problems that are hard to identify; takes time to see change

Philanthropy is a river that runs as an undercurrent throughout our lives. The most important action at the start of your philanthropic journey is entering the stream and getting wet. Start somewhere, with curiosity and compassion, and begin engaging with the problem. Some donors I've worked with staunchly believe that charity-based giving—i.e., give a woman a fish—is the most rewarding and spiritually imperative giving they can do. They believe the metrics and measurements to judge impact in systemic giving deviates from the true purpose of philanthropy. Yet there are those that say teaching a woman to fish is the only way to combat the needs in our community from multiplying. Both of these approaches are valuable when you're informed about the issues and understand your role in the problem and intervention.

There's a fictional story, about a town along a river, that has been used in the social services field which illustrates this duality. People from the town begin to notice babies floating by, and they immediately wade out to save as many as they can from drowning. As the numbers increase and more and more people from the town are required to wade out at all hours of the day and night to gather up the babies, one person asks, "Why are all these babies floating down the river? What is happening?" They step away from their immediate duty of grabbing babies, walk up the bank of the river to see what's going on, and they find a broken bridge. Now, fixing the broken bridge seems to be the ideal solution so that babies stop falling into the river (this would be considered the systemic philanthropic response), but on a very personal level, when you abandon your post at the bottom of the river, someone's child is drowning. In this story we can clearly see that there is space for both responses, and the philanthropic field needs everyone to get involved with what they are particularly passionate about.

Some donors will choose to save drowning babies *today* and some donors will choose to fix the bridge in order to save drowning babies *tomorrow*. Neither is a better response or creates a better philanthropist. Both are attempts to accomplish the same goal. By discovering what you're passionate about, and working with others, you can create a comprehensive framework to respond adequately to the vast challenges we face.

If we take this story a step further, you could pan out and over the river valley to see that all of the bridges are in some state of disrepair. You might conduct a study with locals and government officials to discover that the materials used are shoddy or that there is a war impacting modes of transportation. Every issue you attempt to address is intricately tied to other issues. Being able to flex your vision from minute detail to big picture is a quality that allows for creative solutions and collaborations. I borrow a question from the work of Janine Benyus, a biomimicry science author and designer, when she is encountering a problem with the way something works: *How would nature solve this problem?* Thinking outside of the specific problem you're facing, pulling in ideas from other fields and professionals, is where innovation lies. Understanding how your giving is linked to others, and how it fits within a personally constructed philanthropic plan, is what enables your giving to have maximum power.

Another element to intervening in a system is being aware of where the leverage points are along the spectrum. At some junctures, giving food and shelter is the most important type of philanthropy, while at other times, creating programs that allow people to purchase their own homes is most important. Similar to the housing first model, where advocates are showing that you can impact homelessness by providing people with places to call home, sometimes addressing the "need" level is a direct leverage point to a higher level of intervention. Because when someone is housed, they are no longer homeless. Now you can work with them to move along the spectrum of securing their own future, bringing them into the conversation by addressing the underlying issues.

Of course each case is unique, which makes the whole discussion more challenging. How do you differentiate between a homeless mother of three who is on the streets because of domestic violence and an elderly man who has been struggling with psychosis since his twenties? These are the rich and dynamic conversations that social services and think tanks continue to study, coming up with varying degrees of success. It's why Aristotle says, "To give away money is an easy matter… and in any (wo)man's power. But to decide to whom to give it, and how large and when, for what purpose and how, is neither in every (wo)man's power nor an easy matter." It seems easy, until you start doing it.

I don't have a magic bullet answer, but I do go back to the above definition of *by and with*, rather than *for and to*. Involving those you're trying to help is the only way to ensure sustainable, equitable change both short and long term.

Setting Expectations and an Exit Strategy

The most challenging conversations, at home and at work or anywhere we're creating relationships, seem to stem from misunderstood expectations. In philanthropy, exit strategies are one of the best ways to establish expectations, first with yourself and then with whomever you're making the donation. Most people don't consider exit strategies when they make a gift, and there are many foundations and corporations that don't have them in place either. People tend to give to something until they don't feel like it anymore. They might join another board, start supporting their kid's school, or find that they no longer connect with the mission. Setting expectations and being upfront about exit strategies is essential to intentional philanthropy. Expectations might evolve and change, but the important part is putting thought into it before going in.

In the for-profit world, if you have a successful product or service that is in demand from clients or customers, you have the basic building blocks to make money. In the not-for-profit world, the process of cultivation and donor development is an art precisely because the people you're tapping to pay for a product or service most likely will not directly benefit from that product or service. Much of the work of development staff is creating the story and making the connection for donors to understand that what they're "purchasing" is community resilience, cohesion, and creativity. They have to appeal to our desire to help others and make the case of why this matters.

This relationship of asking and giving is part of the DNA of our philanthropic system, and this system is constructed on a power dynamic. Nonprofits don't have a product to sell and aren't beholden to shareholders per se. They might be doing a fantastic job, and yet donations decline. In fact, I've seen that when nonprofits are doing really well and can begin putting money into a reserve, donors start questioning if they really need the requested donation or grant. If they have "so much" that they're able to save, why would they need additional money? If funders are supporting a startup they might not be as interested when that startup becomes successful. It's a challenge that can be eased by going in with an idea of how long, and at what stage, you'd like to be involved.

This expectation of giving starts first with creating clear intentions for yourself. Do you like funding local startups but not big international organizations? Or further, would you like to provide funding to an individual artist or small business owner? Do you enjoy seeing an organization stabilize and create a sustainable financial model for the future? Would you prefer that all the money go out the door, supporting day-to-day operations? If this is a large and/or recurring gift, or an ongoing gift of time, consider discussing your expectations with those receiving your gift. In order for the gift to actually work for them you need to listen to their expectations and welcome their input as well.

When a nonprofit creates a budget based on the money, time, skills, or networks they've come to expect from you year after year, it can be hard to end that relationship. Development professionals create complex algorithms and donor retention systems to help mediate the ebb and flow of donors to and away from their organization. It's your responsibility to set the limit for yourself, because those taking your gift rarely will set the limit of how much you should give them. How do you do it gracefully, with integrity and goodwill? How do you leave the organization stronger than when you were first introduced? These questions, in fact, are integral to the foundation of being an intentional philanthropist as we dive into the concept of legacy. How do you leave things better than when you arrived? How is the world a better place because you were here?

An exit strategy is a commitment you make to yourself and

other people about the gift you are giving, regardless of what it is. Setting expectations can apply to any of the giving that you're doing. When a couple gets married, their exit strategy comes in the form of a vow that states "until death do us part." That commitment made to each other might need recommitting, but the vows act as a touchstone to come back to and recalibrate the gift of sharing a life. Similarly, if you're set to volunteer at a soup kitchen, you expect there will be someone there to meet you and tell you what needs to be done; and they expect you to stay for your allotted time and to be respectful to clients.

We make these commitments to each other, in large and small ways, and community is built by honoring our commitments. Even if you consider your philanthropy to be minor, only providing little bits of time and money, an exit strategy is a subtle shift that puts you back in the driver's seat of your giving. It also highlights the fact that *giving* is about *partnership*, a relationship you're cultivating with the world around you. Being realistic with what you have available to give, and communicating the boundaries of that giving with those you're serving and supporting, makes the giving authentic and joyful.

As you're designing your philanthropic giving plan, make a note about how long you'd like to support a particular organization (or person, idea, or initiative). Having this exit in mind, you can also be clear when it's time to revise your giving. Do you do an annual review, or do you prefer to go three to five years before reevaluating? For those supporting long-term change it's helpful to put a donation into play that spans several years and spend that time going deeper into the what and how of an organization or initiative, taking the money and time discussion off the table. It allows the relationship between your passion and the passion of those working in the field to come together to create powerful change. Here are some additional questions to consider as you craft your expectations for a strategic giving plan. Jot down your initial thoughts as you read through them.

HOW MUCH

Do you want to set an annual dollar/hour amount to give, or would you prefer to allocate a certain percentage of giving each year (tithing is generally considered 10% of income). Write down your goal for giving:

$_____ per month/year **OR**

_____ % per month/year **AND/OR**

_____ hrs per week/month

Being overcommitted in your philanthropy is similar to any other areas in your life where you overcommit: you don't have the flexibility to respond to something interesting when it shows up. It's nice to include a flexible miscellaneous category to give yourself room to make donations that don't fit in any named category, and in which you can respond to good work and urgent needs that may require a quick reaction. This might be where you'd give to charity runs or natural disasters that occur.

Do you want to have the capacity to give spontaneously? _____

WHERE

Do you want to support organizations, people, and programs in your neighborhood or your city? Or are you drawn to larger state-wide, national, or international programs? Your answer here most likely will be informed by what types of issues you're interested in supporting.

_____ Local

_____ State-wide

_____ National

_____ International

TO WHOM

Would you prefer to support large, well-established organizations or small startups? The smaller, local organizations will feel the impact of a $100 gift much more than the larger, national ones. Being aware of the size of your gifts makes a difference here.

In addition, I consider supporting local artists a part of my philanthropic plan, although obviously this can't be claimed as a charitable gift. Supporting individuals can also be done through scholarships, which can be found at most schools and nonprofits (or you could create your own!).

_____ Large, well-established organizations

_____ Small startups

_____ Individuals

Funding Cycles

Along with an exit strategy, creating a personal funding cycle allows you to give at a regularly scheduled time. The giving is calculated so you don't have to think about it, and you can get to the actual work of it. You might choose to give during the holidays or tax time, as is favored by many people to make the most of tax write-offs. But if this isn't a priority, you can play around with timing.

I've heard of some really dynamic ways of giving back in a scheduled way. Some people use their birthday to make their annual gifts, giving back as an act of gratitude for all they've received over the last year or a way to say thank you for what they hope will be a year of health and happiness ahead. You can "donate" your birthday to a cause and ask friends to contribute on your behalf rather than bring you gifts; several social media sites have jumped on this bandwagon, but beware the processing fees. You could set up a recurring monthly gift, which might allow you to give more than one annual gift ($50 a month out of your paycheck might feel more manageable than a $600 hit in December). I have a friend who hosts an annual gratitude party, where she invites people to submit their favorite charity and bring a financial donation the night of the event. They hold a raffle of sorts where the charity chosen receives the hat of money collected. Everyone who attends learns about all the nonprofits and it creates a special social occasion for potential giving.

There are also large scale funding cycles that you can choose to be a part of. In Washington state, GiveBIG is a one-day online charitable giving event each spring that brings in matching donors and provides "golden tickets" to nonprofits chosen at random. The intent is to increase opportunities for people to donate more and create momentum and celebration around giving back in our community. This is similar to GivingTuesday, the global giving cycle that started in 2012 and takes place on the Tuesday after Thanksgiving to counterbalance the purchasing pull of Black Friday and Cyber Monday (or some might ponder, to capitalize on the advertising and marketing opportunity).

While creating incentives to increase community giving is a good thing, here's my caveat: being swept into a feel-good day of giving once a year can create just another sense of obligation rather than build a foundation of personal philanthropy. As GivingTuesday has gained momentum, I've noticed that it's an opportunity for development professionals at every nonprofit I've had contact with to bombard my inbox with requests for money. It's become an overwhelming contest for attention on just one day. And I've heard from several of these professionals that there is an expectation on their end to participate (from their board of directors, their executive director, other nonprofits or businesses), even though it might not be a part of their annual giving campaign or how they're already cultivating their donors. Giving is a sacred act that starts and ends with relationships, but now there are so many ways to reduce this connection to the transactional click of a button. In this way, the ease of donating holds a positive and a negative: as effortless as paying a bill might make for greater donations on the day of, it won't necessarily connect you to the mission long term or deepen your commitment to philanthropy. This is where your own education and personal work comes in.

So while statistics show GivingTuesday increases donations on that day of the year (there was an astonishing 44% increase in 2017 over the previous year, attributed to the emotionally political landscape at that time), the jury's still out on whether we'll see a similar increase in giving or donor activism spread over the rest of the year. On social media, *the discussion* of GivingTuesday increased on that day and the week preceding, but I haven't seen strong statistics that show how that talking turned to further action. For GivingTuesday to be a truly successful movement, I'd want to see the number of philanthropists grow (and be retained year after year), existing donors increase their annual philanthropy, and most importantly, people begin to develop intentional giving plans that create change to the system.

Now, it is possible that it's the discussion of GivingTuesday, rather than the actual donations, that will create sustainable change to our systems. For example, by creating a counter narrative to the onslaught of purchasing over that holiday weekend we've begun to see pushback on Black Friday and the creation of Small Business Saturday. If that's the case, success won't be clearly evident and change will manifest in a way that makes it difficult to specifically tie back to the movement itself. Changing the status quo takes time, and if money is the only metric with which we track success, we lose sight of the potential success we could have.

What it comes down to is this: when you thoughtfully create your own funding cycles, from recurring annual gifts to one-off special events, you are establishing yourself as a philanthropist by giving of yourself in an intentional way. If you choose to use GivingTuesday (or any other large scale funding opportunities) as part of your funding cycle, my suggestion would be to make it a planned part of your annual philanthropic strategy in order to maximize matching gifts on that day and use it as an opportunity to encourage others to create their own intentional plan for giving.

Strategies for Change

Another way to develop confidence in how your resources are being used is to educate yourself about different change strategies. Do you believe that helping women leave abusive homes starts with shelter, or protection through restraining orders and access to an attorney, or by working with politicians to change the laws protecting women? Or, step way back, would you rather your resources address this issue by going into middle and high schools to work with youth to stop abusers before they grow up? These are all different change strategies addressing the complex problem of domestic violence—and there are many more. Some would argue that in the moment, right here and now, getting that one woman out of her house and sheltered is the number one priority. Others would counter that until we address the cultural and societal issues of abuse we'll be building more emergency shelters, not fewer. Just like babies floating down the river, neither of these responses is wrong, but they focus on different change strategies. Where do *you* want to put your (limited and finite) resources?

Essentially, you are choosing whether you want to work on individual or systemic change strategies, or a combination of the two. Within an individual change theory, you are focused on the day-to-day impacts to individuals. From providing childcare options to low-income working mothers to bringing counseling to addicts living on the streets, individual change strategies impact one-on-one. On the other end of the spectrum, systems change is going to be far more complex, pulling in varying levels of strategies, from research and community convenings to creating shifts in public perception and the status quo. Here is where you might look for an organization that supports pathways for economic opportunities for women or advocates for changing policy around drug use and convictions. If you see the connection between the individual and systems response, you'll want to do further research to find an organization that is capable of managing along the continuum. Being able to employ a multipronged change strategy is challenging and takes a lot more resources, so it's imperative to find an organization that is well versed in systems theory and understands how the whole is greater than the sum of its parts.

You are asking yourself how you want to participate in creating change in your issue of concern, and then finding the right partner who is doing the work well. If the strategies in place make sense to you and feel tangible and doable, you're better equipped to understand when those strategies are successful. You'll come to appreciate that one type of strategy for change might work in a certain scenario but not in another. Scale and context make a huge difference when working on intricate social issues, and where you choose to put your resources depends on what part of the system you're interested in impacting. Understanding this detail adds a powerful component to your philanthropic toolkit.

_____ I am interested in individual change strategies

_____ I am interested in systems change strategies

_____ I am interested in a whole system approach
(combo of individual and systems change)

Overhead and Capacity Building

The basis of any change strategy is overhead and capacity building. These funds provide nonprofits and startup initiatives with the flexibility to create both long-term change and sustainable business models. This philanthropy gives someone the money they need to do what they know is needed and/or supplies them with the resources to take their ideas to the next level. Most funders have become pretty clear supporters of these ideas, but it wasn't always that way, with foundations and major donors directing their gifts to specific programs within an organization. Now I'd say most funders believe that general operating support is one of the smartest ways to invest in organizational sustainability and innovative programming. In *Give Smart*, examples of overhead and its importance to the strength of an organization are outlined:

> Good overhead is a human resource system that helps to develop people and build an organization's managerial bench strength. Good overhead is a functional information technology setup that helps the organization tack its results, learn what's working, and commit more resources in productive directions. Good overhead is a chief operating officer who can take on the responsibility for managing the organization's administrative systems, leaving the executive director free to focus on program issues and developing funding.

In other words, good overhead provides organizations the freedom to get the work done. If you are a philanthropist without a lot of capital, your time and money typically goes to a general operating fund and you might not have given much thought to the idea of "directing" your resources. But it's still worth a bit of discussion because at some point everyone gets caught up in the sex appeal of a specific program and begins thinking about their giving going to something specific within an organization. In reality, the best kind of gift is one that doesn't have strings attached. This is true when donating to an organization or when you're bringing a present to a birthday party. When you find the organization, initiative, or issue you care passionately about, and you believe in the leadership of the organization, their track record, and their vision for change, providing unrestricted general operating support is essential to their long-term success. If you believe in the organization staff enough to provide them with your resources, you should trust that they know where it would best be put to use.

That said, being intentional in your philanthropy also means evaluating the effectiveness of an organization. Trusting staff should come after a bit of informed homework about how the organization is being run. There are many variables (like whether you're donating to a museum or a food bank, whose administration and program finances are going to look wildly different), but generally you'd want to ensure a ratio of 80% program expenses to 20% administration. Of course this will also vary if you're donating to a startup with heavy administration costs upfront, or to many organizations that work systemically who often find it difficult to classify their work as "programs." If you've taken the time to engage with the organization in a meaningful way, by talking to other volunteers or donors, attending events and hearing from those directly impacted, you should get a pretty good sense of this from the work they're accomplishing. There are many resources that provide financial statements for you to do further evaluation, and I encourage this. I've listed several in the resources section. However, it's important to remember that numbers only tell part of the story. Be curious and ask questions before making judgments and attaching strings.

These ideas about how you give, from funding cycles to change strategies, are culled from working with nonprofits, but I believe they can work as well when giving to individuals and deciding which businesses to support. You can research employee benefits and environmental stewardship to make informed decisions about what businesses to frequent. You can review an individual's social justice track record and ask to see a business plan and contemplate their strategy for change. All of these practices are based on acting with intention—clearly outlining your ability and interest in order to set boundaries that both parties are aware of and understand. With every action you create a contract with the world—how you plan to live authentically with your values in place and how you hope to leave a legacy worthy of your time here.

CHAPTER SIX
What You Give

"You cannot get through a single day without having an impact on the world around you. What you do makes a difference, and you have to decide what kind of difference you want to make."

—Jane Goodall

IF BECOMING clear and directed in *how you give* of yourself is the tactical component to intentional philanthropy, understanding *what you give* is the philosophical underbelly. Philosophical because the flip side of what you give is what you *take*, and in order to be intentional with what you give, you have to also reflect on what you receive. These are two sides to the same coin, and accepting this dichotomy opens an inquiry into the difference between enough and too much. It encourages reflection into legacy and forces some tough discussions about money. Anything beyond enough takes up space and weighs us down. It doesn't serve us to be stingy with our time or money or attention—these things are meant to be shared widely. And in sharing them, they come back to us in a myriad of ways. Creating space in our lives by clearing out the clutter of "more" (whether social events, shoes, or salary) sets the stage for different opportunities and experiences to enter. Yet many of us are taking more than we need and giving more than we have, leaving us depleted on both ends of the spectrum. What you give should be based in a realistic assessment of what you have available to give, and this starts with acknowledging the flow of things into and out of your life.

Money and Stuff

According to a study in 2012 by the Chronicle of Philanthropy, the rich gave a smaller share to charity than those poorer (those making $100,000 or more were giving 4.2% while those making between $50,000 and $75,000 were giving 7.6%, and only 2.8% for those making over $200,000). Being a philanthropist is not about the ability to give away millions of dollars, but about giving as much as possible *for you*. What we see is that what is possible for you doesn't directly correlate with having a lot to give. Therefore, understanding your relationship with money is a key pivot point in embracing your role as a philanthropist; because if money is an expression of your life energy and you don't have a good relationship with where it comes from and where it's going, you're essentially squandering yourself.

Making our assumptions explicit about money is powerful. Consider your ideas of money: What does money mean to you? What does money do for you? What would having more or less money look like in your life? Where does your money come from and where does it go?

It's a finite resource, but there might be some "income" that you haven't considered. There's your salary and/or a partner's salary. There's also passive income, like rental property or inheritance. You might make extra money here and there through odd jobs or yard sales. Maybe you get money as gifts during the holidays or on your birthday. This is all money that can be used to buy things. And "things" include your child's education and health insurance for the family. It's used for a mortgage or rent. It's used to buy clothes and haircuts and food. There's a constant flow of money in and out of your life, and this undercurrent creates the foundation of how well we're living. My big aha moment around money came when I realized it wasn't just the money that came in that allowed me to act on my desire to be a philanthropist; it was also the choices I was making about how I spent that money. And while there are legitimately those who do not have enough coming in to live well, if you're reading this book, odds are you have some control here. Many of us have the resources to be more intentional about where our money goes.

It's important to remember that money is a human creation that doesn't exist in nature; it's a tool that allows us to get what we need and what we want. We imbue money with whatever ideas we have about it and it's often abused and misused in our society. Money represents power and prestige because it provides the freedom to do and have whatever you like. And a great deal of money is spent seeking to take our money. Marketing and ad campaigns continually show us what we lack and encourage us to want more of what we don't need. What we're searching for, and what the ad agencies are keenly aware of, is connection and value. So if we establish connection and value aside from money we discover a shift in desires and recognize that what we have available to give increases and expands. Stick with me, this isn't merely wishful thinking.

The women on my retreats go through an exercise where they create two lists: the first is a list of the ten most expensive items they've acquired in the last decade and the second lists the ten items that add the most value to their lives. Of course the first list includes cars and houses and televisions and accessories like shoes and purses and jewelry. With the second list I get stories. I hear about a drawing their child gave them and a dog rescued from the pound and a piece of costume jewelry their grandmother left them. I ask them to go back to the first list and tell me the stories of these items—the meaning behind them. So much of the stuff in the first list includes sentiments of regret, lost time, or worry that things might be mislaid, broken, or stolen. From the second list I hear about relationships, time well spent, calming memories that don't need to be attached to any "thing."

The question that underlies this exercise is, *What brings value to my life?* When you have things around you that don't actively bring you joy (or worse, things that remind you of regret, wasted money, and guilt) you experience an energy suck that permeates your life. When you begin to realize there are things in your life that don't serve you anymore, you can release them and open the door for other possibilities to enter. You begin to see them as mere resources to use, and that they might just be stuck energy in your life. If you've defined your passions and the difference you'd like to make, it becomes clear how to encourage improved flow by finding better uses for these resources.

Try it: Jot down your two top ten lists and think about the stories of these items. It's always a good reminder to pause and reflect on the things in our lives, seeing them with new eyes.

Most expensive items acquired in the last decade	Most valued items acquired in the last decade
1. _____	1. _____
2. _____	2. _____
3. _____	3. _____
4. _____	4. _____
5. _____	5. _____
6. _____	6. _____
7. _____	7. _____

8. _____   8. _____

9. _____   9. _____

10. _____   10. _____

Do you find any overlap on these lists? Notice how you feel when you're looking over them. Are you happy or fearful when you think of them? Do they bring up feelings of control or loss? Consider what items in your home bring emotional value and what would happen if you focused your energy only on those things? Could you let go of the other things? It's an amazing exercise in generosity and attention. Consider what you really need. What's truly important? When I began to make the connection between the "things" in my life and what I'm passionate about, I started to see how I could make a difference with what I already have.

Our life energy, this vital animous that wakes us up each morning, is our most valuable commodity and is the basis of our giving potential. In fact, we use our skills, creativity, and enterprise *to purchase money*; our human capital is the original gold coin. Money is only one expression of our life energy, merely a device we've created to enable a distinct transaction between ourselves and our needs and wants. Only part of our giving is monetized, but this monetized giving is the sliver that gets the most attention. It doesn't come close to accurately or adequately representing what we have available to give that provides value.

When you establish a personal passion to make the world a better place, you want to bring everything you have to the cause. Every resource you have is an expression of your life energy and when you begin to see every aspect of your life as potential giving to this cause, your activities can better align with your desire for a better world. Everything falls into line with the difference you wish to make. When we unleash our giving potential, we bring our whole selves to the table and create a groundswell of powerful philanthropy that elicits change in others as well.

Time and Attention

Once you've begun the process of asking whether the money and stuff in your life adds value, you can put that question to everything you consume: from relationships and food to books and screen time. Everything in your life is a product of your life energy—everything has a cost. Placing the things you consume on the same life energy continuum provides clarity about where you want to place your time and attention.

	LIFE EXPECTANCY AVERAGE REMAINING	
AGE	YEARS	HOURS
20	58.8	515,441
25	54.0	473,364
30	49.3	432,164
35	44.5	390,087
40	39.9	349,763
45	35.3	309,440
50	30.9	270,869
55	26.6	233,176
60	22.5	197,235
65	18.7	163,924
70	15.1	132,367
75	11.9	104,315

The essential guide to this work is the book *Your Money or Your Life* by Vicki Robin and Joe Dominguez. As I read their book, I reevaluated and transformed my understanding of "abundance" into an appreciation of the concept of "enough." I explored my relationship with money and what money represented, which allowed me to recognize that *my time* was *my life energy*, the greatest gift I have to give.

This chart from their book, which is based on actuary tables, plainly lays out how many years and hours you have left to live. It's another exercise I use in the philanthroBE workshops. Each of these hours represents your human capital, the most valuable resource you possess. Find your age in the left-hand column and ask yourself: *How much time do I have left to do what I want to do?*

Large numbers tend to be difficult to visualize, if not impossible to fully grasp. Trying to comprehend forty-four years or 270,869 hours is challenging. On my website at www.kristencorningbedford.com/worksheets you can download a pie chart that will help you create a visual representation of a day in your life and use it to inspire action. Use it to take a look at what one day in your life looks like and reflect on how you're spending your life energy and how it supports your philanthropic intention. Before you can be deliberate with your time, you need to know where it's going.

Once you complete the pie chart, you will get a quick snapshot of how you're spending time. Is this expenditure of life energy in alignment with your values and legacy? Are you spending your days in the ways that you want? If not, why not? What could you be doing differently to support your philanthropic goals?

The logistics of how you spend your time, the 24-hour pie chart, is just the explicit slice you can quantify. Once you're clear about how you're spending your time and if you're spending it on the right things, you can go deeper to ask how you are engaging and paying attention in those moments. Bringing intention to your time creates mindfulness, and mindfulness illuminates the details. It slows you down to allow for insight and pattern and relationship. You might spend every Saturday at the food bank but never learn anyone's name. Or be on the floor playing with your kids while you're thinking through an argument you had at work earlier in the day. Studies continue to show that being present in this way (which is to say, *not* being present) can actually be more damaging to your psyche, making you less happy and less productive. Clifford Nass, coauthor of a 2009 Stanford University study "Cognitive Control in Media Multitaskers," published in the *Proceedings of the National Academy of Sciences*, says, "The research is almost unanimous, which is very rare in social science, and it says that people who chronically multitask show an enormous range of deficits." Matt Killingsworth did his doctoral research at Harvard University on happiness and created an app called Track Your Happiness. Over 5,000 people have signed up to help researchers learn about the causes and correlates of happiness. His TED Talk outlines the results from his years of research and it comes down to a simple truth: we are happiest when we're lost in the moment.

When you offer to volunteer for a couple of hours, put the rest of it on hold for a bit and *be there*. Show up and engage with the people around you. Listen, notice nuance, and enjoy what the opportunity is bringing. Be present with the activity you're engaged in and the people you're with for the time you've allotted. We are more apt to do this when we've clearly set the time aside and created the space to sink into the moment. We teach people how to treat us by setting our boundaries, expectations, and the value of our time. The trick is that we must first do this for ourselves—others won't respect our presence in the moment if we don't respect it for ourselves.

As we pack our days, making plans and staying busy, the

singular moments rush by. I was musing the other day at a stoplight, and bored in my own thoughts for thirty seconds, I instinctively reached for my cell phone to check email. Not so long ago, I would have just sat at the stoplight, listened to music, and watched pedestrians. What free space in our brains are we losing by constantly filling it with static? Mindfulness combats this by bringing us back into our bodies and settling us squarely in our environments. We all have the same number of hours each day, but some people lose time by moving too fast while others sink deeply into the minutes and experience time as it moves. Those people who are present are using their time and attention as a gift, creating a dynamic expression of their philanthropy in the world.

Skills and Strengths | Networks and Influence

Whereas "attention" is the deeper, mindful component of your time, your skills, strengths, networks, and influence add the subtle layers to the value of your time. Again, these can range from knowing how to fix bikes to having a loyal following on Twitter. When you are engaged with the skills and networks that are important to you, the elements that make you unique are highlighted. And this feels good; there's a space made just for you to unlock an important contribution to something bigger than yourself. Bringing intention to these abilities ensures that you further align your time with your values, because seeing your strengths and influence as valuable assets encourages you to fine-tune and cultivate them. You might find you are more protective of the time spent honing these skills and building these networks, because you see how they can be used to benefit people and places outside of yourself.

For me, this realization released me from the guilt associated with the time I spend writing. I have come to recognize, but continually need to remind myself, that creation is what life is all about. It doesn't matter whether you're creating crafts or businesses or children, it's the act of creating that's fundamentally important. So sitting down at the table every day and offering myself as a portal in which to bring forth creation is a sacred and revolutionary act. It is not a selfish indulgence; it is an urgent directive, a meditation, a melting away of self. Writing becomes my prayer for humanity. We all possess this ability and desire to create, and each one of us is a unique entry point for creation to come through. The possibilities of creating real, sustained beauty and change in our world are endless if we each took this directive seriously. We can use our individual creative power to fight for what we care about. Finding and nurturing our gifts so that they can live on in the world is one of the most important things we can bring to bear in the time we have here.

Similarly, consider your networks and spheres of influence. Reflect on who you spend your time with and the kind of person *you are* in relationship with others. When you look back on the 24-hour pie chart and the approximate number of hours you have left, it gets easier to see clearly where you might trim some of the fat. With that comes a closer look at the people and things that are important to you and those that aren't. How do you build on the stuff that works? How do you better connect with the people who bring clarity and light? When you become focused on what you have available to give, and how you're going to make the world a better place, there isn't a lot of room for the people and things that don't also support that passion (not that they have to share the same passion, just that they are supportive of yours). Once you begin clearing out the physical clutter, the mental and emotional clutter will follow. You'll find it easier to dedicate more time to the activities and people that matter.

Finding your authentic self, knowing where you can best

serve, and being present in the presence of others, is the surest way to surround yourself with similarly passionate and compassionate people. You might even uncover skills and strengths you didn't realize you had, and find that you are building on your network. Again, it becomes its own feedback loop: entering the conversation somewhere (that river of philanthropy) is the most important part.

The greatest challenge people have when using their influence and networks to generate support for the issues they're passionate about is that people will give when asked but not necessarily because they're interested in the cause. This creates lots of one-time gifts, but not sustainable gifts over time. I hear this frustration from nonprofits as well. You want your volunteers, donors, and board members to invite their circle of friends and family to attend events and contribute, but this model doesn't necessarily produce long-term donor relationships. How do you ensure your friends don't just follow you to your next interest or project? How can you, as a philanthropic individual, build generous intent in your community that goes beyond the traditional transactional model of "I ask and you give"?

I've considered two possible solutions to this. The first is that by using this book you are focusing your energy and passion and will stick with one or two causes for a much longer timeframe. Ultimately, this keeps your networks interested longer and possibly increases their giving over time. They might also begin to tap their networks and use their influence to expand the donor pool out beyond you. Focusing in helps to magnify your impact by increasing your influence, and it also increases your ability to find the right people to give. Most likely some of the people who had been giving bits of their money and time to support whatever organization you were involved with will drop away. That's totally okay. In fact, that's a good sign you're headed in the right direction. You have to make space for the right people to show up. You might have less of a network by the numbers alone, but the quality of giving should go up. It might take a while, and you could go through a time when you feel like you don't have any influence at all. But if you've created your philanthropic plan of action, it will reemerge stronger, more certain, than ever.

The second solution is actually the result of becoming more intentional about your philanthropy. By narrowing your focus and asking others to join you, you provide them the gift of developing their own joyful giving. Your exploration and strategy in philanthropy should be something you're talking to people about while asking them to donate to the causes you're passionate about. The world needs *philanthropists*, not just donors to this organization or that initiative. As you step confidently into the role of philanthropist, your influence goes beyond cultivating future donors for one specific issue. You are now in a position to use your strength as a philanthropist to create a broader message of giving. Similar to my concerns about GivingTuesday, giving just because someone asks is not, in and of itself, a joyful form of philanthropy. Key to intentional philanthropy is making your own decisions about where you put your energy. Any good fundraiser knows that you pitch your own passion for an issue and ask others to join you, *if they feel the issue resonates with them*. If it doesn't, there should be no pressure for them to give. As you expand awareness about the issues you're passionate about, you can encourage your network to create personal visions and missions for philanthropy in their own lives.

When you honor your passions and focus on living with integrity, you make your torch brighter. It makes me think of the answer Gloria Steinem gave when asked who she's passing her torch to: "…I always say, first of all, that I'm not giving up my torch, thank you very much. But also, I'm using my torch to light other people's torches. Because the idea that there's one torch-passer is part of the bonkers hierarchical idea—and if we each have a torch, there's a lot more light." Use your passion to ignite the passion of the people around you, to strengthen their own torches, their own personal philanthropy. Asking people to support the issues you're passionate about, without asking them to dig deeply into their own passions, is not a sustainable model for change. Bringing more light to the conversation about giving and receiving is the most powerful way to influence your networks. This is how we make the pie bigger.

Make a Difference with What You Have

Underlying all of this discussion of what you give is the reality that you can't give what you don't have. I love this idea from Lynne Twist: "When you let go of trying to get more of what you don't need—which is what we are always trying to get more of—an enormous amount of energy is freed up to make a difference with what you have. When you make a difference with what you have—it expands." By drawing an explicit link between letting go of our desire to get more and our ability to give only what we have available, Twist makes a simple statement about having enough and how the remaining energy to do good reverberates.

Another way to think of this is "giving smarter." The challenge is not to find ways to give *more* but to become *smarter* about your giving, and smarter giving is informed, intentional, and joyful. Giving smarter actually makes *you* smarter because you've entered the feedback loop and are curious about how to interact with the problem. In the book, *Give Smart*, the authors posit that "continuous learning compounds on itself, gradually providing higher 'returns' for a given level of effort. By steadily learning to give smarter, you will be increasing your returns to society through the magic of compounding in much the same manner (albeit without the arithmetic certainty) that $100 at 5 percent interest will exceed $160 in ten years' time." When you create your personal giving plan, you won't necessarily have more to give, but you will witness an expansion in your ability to give.

It's clear that while giving more than you have might make you popular or make you feel good in the short term, it's not sustainable and will leave you anxious for your own security and/or sanity long term. Giving of ourselves is always a balance between our own wants and needs and the needs of the rest of the planet and humanity. Giving too much is just as dangerous as giving too little. Creating an intentional plan for what you have available to give is challenging because it insists that we are realistic with our finite resources. Below are some ideas of simple ways to recognize and appreciate what you already have, and to practice the feeling of having enough.

- Eat food that is locally sourced and in season.
- Join a Buy Nothing group online and start giving things away. Note how it makes you feel.
- Pick one "collection" of things and pare down to a manageable number.
- Clear out your closet and host a clothing exchange with friends.
- Take a social media sabbatical. Let your mind wander when at stoplights.
- Limit multitasking. Start a meditation practice.
- Pay attention when you think or say *I'm not doing enough, If I only had more time, I'm so busy.*
- Embrace imperfection and the integrity of *what is.*

"Let go of trying to get more of what you don't need." "Make a difference with what you have." These statements also support the idea that it's most important to just get started. Stop waiting until you have more money or more time. All you have is today and you have everything you need to make a difference right now. Use some of the simple exercises in awareness above to help create the momentum necessary to address your greater goals in giving and receiving. These baby steps scaffold around you and open up the possibility of ever expansive philanthropy.

You've now explored how to bring intention to your resources. Not merely noting what they are and how to organize and spend them wisely, but actually recognizing how they make you feel and what they bring to your life; in effect asking yourself, how might you and the world make better use of what you have to offer? In her book *Thrive*, Arianna Huffington builds on the David Foster Wallace sentiment that *everybody worships, the only choice being what to worship* by adding, "[a]nd if we worship money, we'll never feel truly abundant. If we worship power, recognition and fame, we'll never feel we have enough. And if we live our lives madly rushing around, trying to find and save time, we'll always find ourselves living in a time famine, frazzled and stressed." To combat the feelings of lack and want, it helps to bring clear focus and intention to your strategies for giving and your available resources. Creating a sustained practice of giving to support an overarching philanthropic vision provides a clear path to deepen our experience of money and time. A future- and outward-focused goal inspires us to align our activities with our passions and convictions, day in and day out.

CHAPTER SEVEN
Creating Your Legacy

"She who knows she has enough is rich."

—Tao Te Ching (paraphrased)

At this point, you've come up with a pretty complex set of guidelines to focus your future giving. You have an idea of a strategy and maybe even some new ways of thinking about what you'd like to give to the world. Now comes, what I consider to be, the best part. In this final section, you get to dream of what your giving makes possible. Visualizing and verbalizing your legacy is a personal journey, and the construction of it can be empowering and rewarding, not only in your philanthropy but in all areas of your life. Your legacy is the story you will leave behind, and being intentional with it while you're alive is powerful medicine for the world.

At some point in your life you might begin to consider how you want to be remembered. You might ask yourself, *What is the purpose of my time on this planet? What is the purpose of any of our time here?* Some people never fully come into the question of why they're here and what the purpose is. Others are born with it tattooed across their heart. This questioning doesn't necessarily correlate with age either—you might be eighty and never considered the truth of your life while a twelve-year-old might already have developed a keen sense of her life horizon. You are never too young to contemplate your legacy. Discovering what you have to offer, and what you enjoy giving to others, is the key to unlocking the needs in our communities.

Like the concept of philanthropy, *legacy* can feel like something wealthy, well-connected people talk about. And because talking about legacy inherently involves an acknowledgment of death, most people don't like to think too much about it. Yet we all deserve to know how our actions will impact the future story of our planet. Making the decision to know and craft your legacy is an important moment: in it you recognize that your wealth is not determined by what you have, but by what you give away. It also requires a commitment to something larger than yourself. We will all leave a legacy of some sort, and by becoming directed and strategic you ensure this legacy is also positive and joyful, both now while you're alive and for others after you're gone.

Your Vision for a Better World

"...[I]n creating a vision, we are creating a power, not a place; an influence, not a destination. Now we need to imagine ourselves as beacon, towers of information, standing tall in the integrity of what we say, pulsing out congruent messages everywhere. We need all of us out there, stating, clarifying, reflecting, modeling, filling all of space with the messages we care about. If we do that, a powerful field develops—and with it, the wonderous capacity to organize into coherent, capable form."
—Margaret J. Wheatley, *Leadership and the New Science*

On Whidbey Island there is a retreat center called The Whidbey Institute. It's where I've hosted my weekend retreats for women philanthropists because the atmosphere and energy there encompass the ideals of feminist philanthropy: that people are informed, intentional, and joyful. They run a gamut of events and retreats and sit on one hundred acres of old growth forests that are open to the public. It's a great place to visit if you find yourself around Langley, Washington.

They also have a lovely labyrinth on the property that I use for our legacy exercise. Many women are anxious about walking the labyrinth, confusing it with a maze that they'll get lost in. But a labyrinth is a walking meditation, a path based on nature's spirals. It's an ancient practice found around the world to reduce stress and quiet the mind. There is only one path in and out, traveling to the center and back again, with no dead ends.

As you explore your legacy, I encourage you to find a labyrinth to walk. You can find labyrinths in parks, schools, and church parking lots. I was surprised to discover a labyrinth painted on the playground at the public school down the street from our house. Generally the path leads you along the outside, starting wide and slowly bringing your brain into focus as you approach the center. Once you reach the middle, pause for a minute in order to let your quiet mind receive whatever pops into your head. Then return the way you came in, meditating on the message from the center (which is *your* core) in order to take it back out into the world. This meditation doesn't work for everyone (one woman told me she jumped right to the center and then jumped back out and into the woods for a run). But for many women it is incredibly useful. One woman, who was the most vocally hesitant and skeptical, decided she liked it so much she went back out, by herself, in the middle of the night with a headlamp to walk it again! There is no right way or wrong way to do it, however if you find a labyrinth isn't right for you, or you can't locate one close to you, you can simply go for a walk or sit quietly. There is something powerful about focused walking meditations, especially in nature. It's a way to connect the head and the heart.

Quiet your mind in order to consider the following questions:
- *How will my being here leave the world a better place?*
- *What gift do I bring to the world?*
- *What if I realized my vision? How would the world around me look different?*

These are big, important questions. Take your time with them. The answers you are nurturing will create context and depth in everything you do. Consider the values and passions you established in the previous section. You'll see that these play throughout your thinking, as well as the resources you have available to give. This part is about dreaming and imagining. You are not bound by *what is*. Use this meditation to discover audacious possibilities to the question, *What do I want for the world?*

Allow yourself to go wherever your heart and mind take you, without judgment. This is harder than it appears. We are programmed to criticize that little voice that tells us it might want something outside of the norm. We bury it so deeply that we forget what it sounds like when we hear it. Sometimes it's a simple phrase like "show up." Once during the labyrinth meditation I received the message, "If you walk the path regularly you'll understand the pattern…which is different from solving the pattern." I understood this on the tangible level (walking the labyrinth regularly you'd most likely get to know the pattern of the path pretty well) but I also heard a deeper meaning behind the instruction (enjoying the walk and being regularly present "in it," aka life, without desperately trying to understand it, might be the only real way to embrace it). The task here is just to listen and take note. You might hear something ridiculous. Go with it. Give yourself over to the possibility of discovering something new about yourself. It takes great personal trust and integrity to let that voice guide you.

Once you've concentrated on the answers to the above

questions, find some space to daydream a response to the following event:

It's an evening many years into the future. You're receiving recognition for your work achieving some goal as it pertains to one, or all three, of the passions you highlighted earlier in the book. You are being honored for your role as a philanthropist. This award might be coming from a local nonprofit you've been working with, your alma mater, or the neighborhood kids. Maybe it's coming from the president of the United States or it's a toast being made by a family member at a simple holiday meal. Whether the award is small or large, you are deeply touched as this gesture is a testament to your passion and the change that has taken place because of your involvement.

First, tell us a little bit about what you did: What have you accomplished? How did you do it? Who helped you? How do you feel about it? You could also ponder where you were surprised on this journey. Where were you joyful? Where did you struggle? Write up some background in an acceptance speech you'll make the night of this event. You're providing the audience this evening with a recap of your work, a reflection of your experience.

Now, create a vision of this better world. Your accomplishment has made a difference and it's noticeable. Really see this world, flesh it out. Close your eyes and imagine it. Remember, this is say, ten to thirty years from now. What sounds do you hear? What clothes are you and your friends wearing? Who are you surrounded by? How are some of your day-to-day activities affected? How has this impacted your neighbors and wider community? Take a minute to imagine it. Jot down some of these images or words.

Finally, once you've constructed a solid picture of this future event, consider what piece of this vision is most exciting to you. Where is your energy in the picture you just painted?

Creating a detailed account of an ideal future reality, including the role you played bringing it about, forms a dynamic starting place. When you discover where your energy is in the above described future, it makes it easier to get involved and sustain that involvement through challenging times. Your energy, that life force we've been talking about, is a potent driver of change. When you light upon the thing you are powerfully passionate about, it becomes easier to channel all of your resources to support it.

Most often we set a goal and then create steps to reach the goal, without first making the goal real in our heads. Working backward this way, naming the reality and "looking back" to see what got us there, changes the way we think about it from obscure to concrete. You've named your challenges and successes before you actually encounter them, down to what you wore the night of the celebration event. The path to success is doable, merely by the fact that in your mind, it's already been done. When you actually encounter challenges and successes, whether similar to the ones you envisioned or not, your body recognizes them and makes them less threatening. Conquering the fear of failure and success is almost always more difficult than conquering the real thing.

The strength in this visioning exercise comes from making your assumptions explicit and highlighting unintended outcomes. When you process a desired outcome this way, backward from completion to the steps it took to get there, you are reverse engineering your vision. You are taking apart something that's already been completed (even if only in your mind) to see the intricacies of how it works in order to enhance the effort when you undertake it in real life. In some ways, these steps are helping you to develop a personal theory of change, which is to say, you are naming your long-term goal, working backward in time to uncover the outcomes necessary to illustrate progress along the way, and only through this process discovering what interventions will work to achieve the goal.

Your vision identifies the key stakeholders, the potential challenges and successes, and the desired outcomes along the way.

Your Intention and Action Steps

Just as you made the expectations about your desired future explicit, naming your intention is a way to put a stake in the sand in order to know your truth completely without reservation. Intentions should be simple; in fact, they're meant to be short and sweet. When you base your actions on a defined statement of intent, it becomes easier to be intentional with everything else. Remember, you are charting a direction, not a final destination. This is the starting point as well as the place that holds the grand vision together.

After establishing your values, highlighting the issues you're passionate about, and crafting a vision for the future that you want to be integral in creating, you can sum it all up pretty concretely in a single statement of intent. After less than twenty-four hours together, the women who attend my retreats come up with incredible intentions, and I've heard back from many of them that they immediately begin living more earnestly in pursuit of these. Here are a few of these statements of intent:

- I want to transform the human relationship with water.
- I want to create whole adults by teaching to all parts of a young child.
- I want to transform fear of differences into celebrations of diversity.
- I want to joyfully foster and support a wonderfully caring community.

These are bold statements! The action words alone are powerful: *transform, create, foster*. These intentions propose something big for these women to sink their teeth into and build a life around, a wide container to fill with all sorts of possibilities. Within these statements, all components of a life can rise to the challenge. All essential activities, from where you shop to how you travel, from who you spend your time with to how you interact with the woman behind the counter at the post office, can align with supporting your true intent in making the world a better place. This is the crux of who you are. You should recognize yourself in your intention statement. It should feel like settling into a comfortable chair.

Take all that you've been working on so far and write out your statement of intent. Don't get too hung up on a forever statement, as it could change through the years. Simply consider what you want to do *right now*. It might surprise you to find as you come back to it over the years that, in fact, it does essentially stay the same. But for today, ask yourself, *What do I want to do?*

I want to _____

_____

_____

_____

Many years ago, while I was working on my master's degree, I created a statement to direct my learning and support my thesis. I was in the middle of creating a nonprofit to serve young women and I knew that it was merely a stepping stone to something bigger; my dream was more political in nature, more systemic. My vision for the organization was broader than providing formal wear to high school girls. I stated, **I want to facilitate authentic experience and communication between generations of women in order to honor the story of the individual as a means to strengthen society.** When I left the nonprofit in the capable hands of my cofounder and took a job at the Community Foundation in Pierce County, I put the intention statement aside. But it began to bubble up again when I left that job to stay home full-time with my newborn son and was trying to figure out what I might do next. I wrote, **I want to host simplicity retreats, focused on women and girls finding the space they need to create the lives they want for themselves, their communities, and this world**. With this second statement I launched the philanthroBE retreats. It wasn't until one of the attendees in the second year asked me about my statement of intent that I was reminded of that first statement, and in comparing them realized that they held very similar sentiments about authenticity and community and relationship.

Once this statement is written down you'll be amazed how it will begin to show up in your life. Even when you put it aside and perhaps begin down another path, it's fascinating to revisit it and recognize that you've been working toward it all along. This thing that you value, that you hold dear, that you are passionate about—this thing lives in your heart. Sometimes our brains forget. Sometimes we're driven toward money and prestige, or responsibility or duty. But our hearts never forget what truly matters, and what truly matters pushes up through the cracks in the pavement of our abandoned playgrounds.

To combat some of this forgetfulness you can write down a short list of action items you pledge to take over the next year that will move you toward the goal. These steps should be manageable, as they are meant to create movement, not accomplish the goal itself. During one retreat, one woman's action item was to call the local children's hospital to ask about volunteering. Another was going to sign up for a mediation course. Another was going to simply research the geographic region in our state that she was interested in protecting (and before the night was over she was curled up in a quiet corner getting started). All of these were tangible and slowly moved the women toward action. And action begets greater action. In addition, you never know when these singular steps will open doors to something beyond what you'd originally imagined. The woman who began her research the evening of the retreat found herself at a party later that year talking to someone who she quickly realized was speaking about the same issues she was interested in. Because she'd done the research to better understand the issue, the other person recognized her as a knowledgeable advocate and asked if she'd like to get more involved.

There are a couple of things you can do to keep yourself accountable. Ideally, you'd be able to find a working partner or a group of people who you can share this journey with. Sharing your goals with each other and having others to check in with and support is an important piece of accountability. If you don't have someone to share with directly, you could declare your intention statement on social media. Posting this type of goal for the world to see is powerfully motivating. I also have my retreat participants write themselves a letter that I collect and then mail back to them six months after the retreat. This letter serves as your own personal reminder of the passion you felt when you initially created the goal. It's the message from your heart reminding your brain that it has a goal that must be acknowledged. Tuck the letter somewhere out of the way and set a reminder on your calendar for six months from now to dig it up and read it.

Action steps for the year   **Date/Month**

1. _____ _____

2. _____ _____

3. _____ _____

You're developing your philanthropic operating system, the framework in which you place your giving and the structure that dictates how you spend your resources. This is an integral step in aligning your values with your actions. And aligning what you value with how you act creates a life of integrity and balance.

Your Philanthropic Purpose

Writing out a philanthropic purpose statement provides a touchstone when you're asked to donate your time or money, to give gifts, or when you go shopping. When you are clear about your purpose and how you want to make the world a better place, moving through life making decisions about how you spend your time and money becomes integral to who you are. You are living as an informed consumer, intentional and joyful in how you give of yourself.

A philanthropic purpose statement lays out your giving philosophy. It highlights why something is important to you and who and/or what will benefit from your giving. It can also include *what* you give (the multiple resources you possess) and *how* you do it (timing and level of engagement). Writing a philanthropic mission statement sets and engages your intention for action. The basis of this is your statement of intent (*I want to...*), which you've already written. Now round that sentence out by adding, *For whom? Why? How? What?*

You might support your statement with information about a family history with this issue ("because my aunt escaped domestic abuse" or "because my son has food allergies"), with the ways you'll give ("5% of pretax income" or "two hours a week" or "through a bequest"), and a timeline, ("I'll stick to this plan for the next year and reevaluate." or "I will prioritize this giving for at least six years, in conjunction with my board service"). You could also include a personal statement of belief, such as, "I believe that people have final say on what happens to their bodies, therefore I want to ensure that every woman has the right to choose when to start a family and has the resources available to do so."

You might choose to include further clarification for your intent, making a very specific direction for what you want your money/time/skills to support. You could include clarifying details like levels of intervention (direct services or advocacy) or change strategies (individual or systems), or some characteristics (innovative, socially responsible, intergenerational, self-sustaining) of the type of organization, initiative, or person you'd like to fund. There might also be a desire to include something like "I want my gifts to challenge the community to leverage their own giving."

Below are some examples of how each of the above intentions might become individual philanthropic purpose statements that can help as you craft your own.

I want to transform the human relationship with water. I do this by volunteering ten hours a month to protect the Cedar River Watershed, and advocating on its behalf. I donate money to a national agency committed to protecting individual rights to clean water, which will also receive a bequest through my will. I have installed rain barrels in my yard and will volunteer to teach others how to do this.

I want to create whole adults by teaching to all parts of a young child. I believe it's easier to build up a child than to repair an adult. I dedicate my volunteer time to our preschool, and use my legal background to advocate for early childhood education at the state level. I am committed to setting up a scholarship in honor of my late mother, who was a lifelong educator. My partner and I have committed to one of us being a stay-at-home parent, at least for the next five years, at which point we will reevaluate.

I want to transform fear of differences into celebrations of diversity. I come from a biracial family and have experienced the loneliness of being excluded because of fear. I fund organizations working to create conversations across racial divides, particularly ones that intersect with government agencies. In addition, I donate 10% of my time as a diversity consultant to nonprofits wishing to provide a more equitable and inclusive experience for their employees and clients.

I want to joyfully foster and support a wonderfully caring community. I am passionate about end-of-life care and support organizations who are transforming the experience of aging and death. Currently, I sit on the board of a local hospice program that helps people stay in their homes, finding ways to connect them to their families and each other. I use my professional skills on the grants committee and volunteer at their annual gala. I also advocate for elder care and raise awareness of elder abuse. I am exploring the idea of becoming a death doula!

In crafting this philanthropic purpose, you can take your intention a step further by changing the tense from future to present: *I want to transform the human relationship with water* becomes *I transform the human relationship with water*. *I want to create whole adults by teaching to all parts of a young child* becomes *I create whole adults by teaching to all parts of a young child*. Again, this is an opportunity to play with how your mind visualizes your challenges and successes, and ultimately what actions you'll take. If your statement is current, it directs your actions from doing to being. This statement is now alive in your life in a new way. Your statement no longer asks how you're going to do it, but opens up the much more dynamic and powerful question about how you are currently doing it. This iteration immediately places you in the picture, and from there, you can build an entirely different framework for giving.

R. Buckminster Fuller embedded his philanthropic purpose in his personal mission, which he dedicated his life to, in the following quote: "We are called to be architects of the future, not its victims. The challenge is to make the world work for 100% of humanity in the shortest possible time, with spontaneous cooperation and without ecological damage or disadvantage of anyone. How can we make the world work for 100% of humanity in the shortest possible time through spontaneous cooperation without ecological damage or disadvantage to anyone?" Be like Bucky: try rephrasing your philanthropic mission statement as a question. Questions tap into our curiosity because they seek answers and create challenges, which means they can illicit new ideas. Try it: reframe your philanthropic purpose statement into a question and see what emerges.

PART THREE | BE JOYFUL

Once upon a time, when women were birds, there was the simple understanding that to sing at dawn and to sing at dusk was to heal the world through joy. The birds still remember what we have forgotten, that the world is meant to be celebrated.

—Terry Tempest Williams, *When Women Were Birds*

JOY IS at once transcendent and grounding: a flash of awareness and the calm knowledge that all the world needs is your presence and appreciation. In a moment of joy, you realize you already have everything you need and are overcome with the feeling that *this*, watching the sunset, ants on the sidewalk, a baby taking his first steps, the death of someone you love, *is enough*. Joy contains the hope, thankfulness, and awe that humbles you by pulling back the gauze of the everyday in order to see the spaces in between, those little graces that live just out of sight when you're going about your scheduled day. This is why *joy* is the action word to propel modern-day philanthropists into a new era of giving.

Joyful philanthropy is not rooted in anger or fear, helplessness or obligation, which are the drivers of transaction and do not question the status quo. Joyful giving expresses intricate feelings of gratitude and beauty, which supports transformation. This is powerful because joy, and therefore joyful philanthropy, holds a bittersweet expression of all that is and all that can't be, of all that came before and all that lies ahead. It acknowledges what George Vaillant, a psychiatrist and professor at Harvard Medical School, succinctly points out in Jennifer Senior's book *All Joy and No Fun*: that "joy is grief inside out." Philanthropists engaging in joyful giving and receiving are taking the muck around them and transforming it. They are using their own personal stories and listening intently to the sorrows of others.

All around us the world teaches duality: good and evil, light and dark, male and female, sky and earth. Joy is one side of the coin of life, while grief is the other. Yet there is a place on the edge where both exist at once, where there are smudges of the twin, like the dot in the yin of yang. This is the liminal space that opens to engaged, compassionate, smart, and entrepreneurial philanthropists. Wrapped tightly around melancholia, joy is the antidote to grief. Those that know this can play with the world and its complexities. Your giving potential is defined by understanding grief and engaging with joy anyway.

So while the first two sections created a framework to help nail down the specifics of what, when, where, and how you give, this section is more philosophical. It asks you to fold your philanthropy into your day-to-day life. In these next pages you are invited to go deeper and explore what a life of joyful giving and receiving might look and feel like for you. When you create a practice of gratitude, simplicity, and engagement you begin to transform your experience of life itself.

And this is the ultimate work of a philanthropist: all actions promote a love for humanity. And a love for humanity in action, with humility and compassion, is social justice. This type of philanthropy demands a higher level of responsibility and accountability. It is personal and political, and it constantly calls you to transform your relationship to yourself and the world.

CHAPTER EIGHT
Gratitude

"Saying and meaning 'Thanks' leads to a crazy thought: What more can I give?"

—Anne Lamott, *Help Thanks Wow*

AT THE start of the book I said that if you find your joy you will find your generosity. And this is true—if you discover what brings you happiness and contributes to a deeply held passion, it will become increasingly easy to be generous. For me, becoming a parent created a monumental shift in recognizing and nurturing my generosity, but this expansion of the experience of giving and receiving can come through any activity you care deeply about. There are many entry points to selflessness. Any action or activity that allows you to see all the moving pieces that incorporate the joy and grief spectrum will push you toward your generosity horizon.

Yet finding our joy is not quite as simple as discovering our passions, as we did in Section Two. Having passion for our life or our work doesn't necessarily guarantee joy. In fact, joy flickers on and off, episodically available and unavailable during our lives. That's because this elemental component of living thrives on an appreciation for the richly layered experience of living, serving as a sparkplug of sorts, animating the drive of desire. This appreciation of life is the seed of joy, and the thing that must be nurtured in order to cultivate generosity. Without this seed of joy, our passion can falter. As Benedictine monk David Steindl-Rast says, "The root of joy is gratefulness.... It is not joy that makes us grateful; it is gratitude that makes us joyful." So if being grateful makes us joyful, and being joyful strengthens our generosity, it's clear that being grateful is also the seed of generosity. Gratitude, joy, and generosity live along the same circular path, supporting the sustained experience of each other. To be joyful in giving and receiving means to first be thankful for what you have and what you have to give. So although generosity is a natural outgrowth of being joyful, you can find joy through your generosity as well. The fulcrum on which both of these rest, however, is gratitude.

Gratitude nurtures the work of the philanthropist because it strengthens the foundation of giving and receiving *with intention.* This giving comes from a place of appreciation for what we have. It makes us humble and provides perspective. It encourages simplicity and opens our eyes to beauty. When we talk about gratitude, we're really talking about life itself. Being thankful for the world around us, however it manifests in each evolving moment, is nestled into the deepest gratitude for the gift of our lives, the space between the day we were born and the day we die. Research is beginning to prove that gratitude isn't just something nice to do, it makes our lives better. "Gratitude is literally one of the few things that can measurably change peoples' lives," writes Dr. Robert A. Emmons in his book *Thanks!*, where he details the first major study of gratitude. His research found that people who listed five things they were grateful for each week were 25% happier—they were more optimistic about the future, felt better about their current situations, and exercised more each week than those in the control groups.

Additional research is discovering that people who practice

gratitude consistently report a plethora of health and social benefits, like stronger immune systems, feeling less lonely and isolated, and acting with more compassion and generosity. Psychologist Dr. Jeffrey Froh summarizes the practice of gratitude by stating, "As gratitude involves wanting what one has rather than having what one wants, instilling a sense of gratitude may help people appreciate the gifts of the moment and experience freedom from past regrets and future anxieties." Gratitude is a personal perspective, an appreciation for *what is*. When you are grateful, you open yourself to the possibility of something beyond the immediate concrete experience of good and bad. Essentially, being grateful is saying, "yes, *and*," accepting whatever might come, and responding, "Why thank you. What can I do with this?"

"Yes, *and*" is also a theatre improv game which sharpens an actor's ability to take whatever is lobbed at them and roll with it. Really good improv artists do more than pick up where the ball landed, they take it to the next level. They are joyful in the possibly bizarre scenario they've been handed. They stroll right up to it and through it, gracefully take the baton and use the suggestion to construct a wildly plausible new reality. Practicing gratitude is similar to improv in this respect because when you are practicing gratitude, you acknowledge that the world is intrinsically good (that there are no bad suggestions, only how you respond) even on those days when it doesn't feel like it. You know those days: when you leave your coffee on top of the car, or the boss passes you over for a promotion, or the kids draw on the walls. The day your mother dies, or you read in the paper about hurricanes, tsunamis, and earthquakes, or planes being shot out of the sky. I can feel my chest tighten at the thought of any of these things happening—and they are happening all over the world. *Life* is improv. Being grateful for what you *do have* allows you to say, "Yes, this is all happening, *and* I choose to take this information and make something beautiful and necessary from it." We all have the creativity to elevate the scene we're in into something interesting and inspiring.

And though the act of being grateful in and of itself won't alleviate concrete suffering, the simple practice of gratitude does create an internal momentum that promotes action. Gratitude isn't going to save your house from refinance or keep your children safe. On its own, gratitude can't combat great loss and the atrocities of war and hatred. But gratitude does reframe the situation, providing a broader perspective in which joy can creep in. For the philanthropist, gratitude increases the joy with which to tackle some of the toughest challenges humanity faces. Addressing these systemic difficulties without joy makes it increasingly easy to succumb to depression, anxiety, and apathy, which serves to chokehold your ability to be generous. Gratitude is an approach to life that doesn't sugarcoat or minimize the challenges, but applies a varnish that both coaxes out the unique rough edges and the water stains.

Exploring and highlighting the dark nooks and crannies in life, while maintaining a stance of gratitude, allows us to appreciate the gift within the pain. Dr. Viktor Frankl, Austrian neurologist and psychiatrist who survived the Nazi concentration camps, eloquently expressed this when he said: "We must never forget that we may also find meaning in life even when confronted with a hopeless situation, when facing a fate that cannot be changed. For what then matters is to bear witness to the uniquely human potential at its best, which is to transform a personal tragedy into a triumph, to turn one's predicament into a human achievement. When we are no longer able to change a situation…we are challenged to change ourselves." Having gratitude acknowledges hopelessness and tragedy and yet gives way to wonder. It challenges us to be the change we wish to see in the world, because systemic change always starts at home. Our experience of life is the only thing we can ever truly change, but imagine if that was happening the world over. The slogan *think globally, act locally* is talking about *you* on the minutest of scales. *You* are the most local you can get. Consider the system, then change your role in it.

While some might think it feels inauthentic to be grateful when there is so much pain and destruction around us, expressing thanks for what you have isn't the same as wallowing in your privilege. Being grateful shouldn't make it easy for you to look away. It isn't about feeling better than someone else because you have more than they do, or because you've been given something they haven't. Gratitude is a practice, not a destination. It's acknowledging the gift and paying respect to the blessing of having received it. Being grateful opens your heart to the knowledge that gifts come and go, that you have received today in order to give tomorrow. Being grateful, then, is a cure to indifference and sorrow. And finding things to be thankful for in the face of anger and evil is a form of activism. It transforms your experiences into lessons and opportunities for growth by taking back the power of injustice and inequity. Just grasping on to one singular nugget of thanks can alter the course of action. It stops the fast-paced flow of life so that you can witness the privilege of being you, in this particular moment, at this particular time.

Consider your current circumstances. What are you grateful for right now?

Strengthening the muscle of the generous heart starts with giving thanks. Dr. Emmons has several evidence-based ideas for developing a gratitude practice, and like anything worth doing, they require discipline and commitment. I've noted a few of them that have been beneficial for me, and you can find a more comprehensive list in his book. The benefits of gratitude are well studied and form the basis of authentic philanthropy, so I encourage you to find a way to make a daily practice of gratitude work for you.

Start a gratitude journal. During a rough time in my life over a decade ago I began journaling one thing I was thankful for every day. I kept the journal by my bed and made it something I did before going to sleep. Start wherever you are (which might mean writing "I'm thankful the day is over") but find something new each day to be grateful for and reflect on these items, people or experiences as gifts. I came across that journal recently and it was a fascinating look into a time when ever so slowly life began to open itself to receive gifts rather than expect perfection.

Post a quote about giving and the web of life. Make it a quote that resonates with you, and place it somewhere you will see it every day. Maybe at the back door or on the mirror of the bathroom. I've painted William Blake's line, *eternity is in love with the creations of time*, across a large sepia photo of my grandparents to remind me that everything is ephemeral and each of us stands as witness to creation and all that is, is all that is meant to be, and that the whole system is joyful at the thought of it. This daily reflection on a quote or statement reinforces your ability to recognize that the gift of your life is owed to something outside of yourself. I've included many quotes throughout this book, and you can find hundreds more in religious and secular and scientific communities.

Take a walk…in the woods. In Japan, there is a practice called forest bathing, or shinrin-yoju. Essentially, it's bathing in the forest atmosphere, and it's considered medicinal for combatting stress and anxiety. It is not exercise or hiking, it's walking slowly among trees, using all of your senses to engage with and experience nature. Taking time out to breathe in the world around you intensifies your appreciation for all that is.

If you live in the city, it can be challenging to find forests to walk through. You can go to a park or spend time in your garden and reap similar benefits. The goal is to be in your body (without distractions like cell phones), surrounded by trees.

Recognize yourself in the dance of giving and receiving. View the continuum of giving and your role in giving to others and receiving from others. Take this a step further and reflect on what troubles you've caused to others, either through your thoughts or actions. By acknowledging how your actions have caused suffering, you can appreciate the grace with which others have given you the gift of acceptance and forgiveness. Being a flawed human being is part of our humanity; mistakes are part of our growth and learning, and showing kindness to others as they grow and learn is a great gift. You might get really introspective and turn this kindness toward yourself and practice this dance internally.

Reframe what and who you are grateful for. Ask yourself to be thankful to people or situations that have hurt you or made you uncomfortable. Reconsider who is actually giving and who is receiving in your interactions. When we found our house had been broken into one evening after work, my husband and I considered the life of the person who robbed us and sent blessings to them, that they got what they needed by selling the things they stole. We were scared and angry, but we had our health, the ability to go out for dinner, a job to go to the next day, family to support us if things got bad. In that moment we shifted our thinking and realized the taking was also a gift that slowed us down and caused us to reflect on all that we had to be thankful for. Consider similar reframes: Are you grateful to the woman on the street asking for money or food? Being thankful for her shifts your giving to one done out of joy. And your joyful interaction might be more of a gift than you realize. I once was chatting with a man in line at a coffee shop when I noticed the large pack at his feet and the rough and dirty hands he extended out to greet me. The barista started to shoo him away with a free refill, shaking his head in apology to me for the intrusion. As I wheeled the stroller toward the door this man called out, "Thank you for letting me say hello to you." I'll never forget it. Who's to say what others might need in a particular moment and what you're able to give just by being present and kind. Who's to say what you might receive in return.

Share your gratitude and generosity: talk about it! My family goes around the table at dinner to share what each of us is thankful for that day in lieu of a formal grace. Sometimes we include how we gave of ourselves by helping others. We hear about new friends and gardening adventures, about creative problem solving and schoolyard antics. My hope is that our family dinnertime conversations will evolve as the boys get older to further engage with the spectrum of giving and receiving, encouraging them to be vulnerable and ask for help when they need it, and finding ways to act as change agents on a daily basis.

Research is proving that we have greater influence on our children's giving when we *talk with them* about philanthropy instead of relying on role-modeling alone. Making a daily practice of discussing our role as givers and receivers helps young people make the connection between how their actions impact the world around them. And this is true for our wider circle of influence as well. Being a philanthropic role model by volunteering and hosting tables and donating is not as impactful as talking to people about your philanthropy. Make the implicit explicit by sharing the commitments you're making, how you're giving of yourself, and why. Your stories of gratitude and giving inspire others to make their giving personal.

Removing Barriers to Gratitude

"In the end, we'll all become stories."
—Margaret Atwood, *Moral Disorder*

Of course, it's not always easy to be thankful. Everywhere we look in our consumer society we're reminded that we could be doing better and we could be doing more. Even when we're aware of it, it's hard to heal from it. Our wants and desires are black holes that need constant sacrifice; it's simply the culture we're cooked in. The consumer mentality is a direct assault on being thankful for what we already have, and this in turn inhibits our ability to give and receive joyfully.

So how do we remain content with what we have and stop comparing ourselves to others? How do we deepen our respect for what is and see the pattern that connects the parts to each other and the whole? The solution is not so simple as to stop focusing on wanting more, because what you focus on grows. Trying to merely remove the barriers to gratitude is a surefire way to entrench them. When you tell a toddler they can't have something it piques their interest in the forbidden item; instead you demonstrate what they *can* have or do. We all have a toddler brain when it comes to retraining ourselves to want less and appreciate what we have. Supporting a practice of gratitude means changing larger patterns in our lives: when we create experiences, practice mindfulness, and take care of our own needs, we choose story over stuff.

Creating Experiences

Researchers have studied the difference in satisfaction between purchasing a material item and purchasing an experience and found that while the satisfaction and happiness at the point of purchase were about the same (people are excited by the newness of something different), once this novelty wore off the pleasure of the material item began to decrease, while the enjoyment gained from the experience grew. There are three reasons attributed to this, as Thomas Gilovich of Cornell University outlines. First, experiences yield better stories. Think about the exercise in Section Two comparing your most expensive versus most valued possessions. Often in conversation about these lists people find they have had to put down intangibles like experiences and relationships for their most valuable possessions. These are things that couldn't be quantified by a bank.

One of the best gifts my husband gave me, the week before our wedding, was tickets to the Treasure Island Music Festival in San Francisco to see Modest Mouse perform. He'd been told it was traditional to get his bride-to-be a piece of jewelry, but instead we spent a day listening to music, drinking beer, watching the lights of the Bay Bridge appear as night fell, and finding a tiny hole-in-the-wall Chinese restaurant near our hotel at one in the morning. It was as extravagant as a pearl necklace, but this memory of spontaneous adventure has become a bigger part of who I am. I think back on this day often, a blip in our history together, but a reminder of life before we started the journey toward PTA meetings and folding endless laundry and helping our aging parents.

Which is the second reason experiences bring great satisfaction: experiences make you distinctly you. They remind you of past iterations of yourself, and provide a mini vacation whenever they're remembered. They shape who you are by providing opportunities for growth and connection to yourself. Experiences are truly the gifts that continue to give the more they are used. A memory can be given away in the telling, over and over, whereas a pearl necklace becomes an heirloom that can only be given away once. Building on this, the third reason your enjoyment of experiences grows after the point of purchase is that these stories provide a springboard to better connection to others. You have interests and passions and experiences to talk about, and you can share these with new people in order to form relationships and deepen bonds. Your gratitude grows when you make choices that open you to story and deepen your experience of yourself and your relationships with others.

Practicing Mindfulness

In those moments when I've lost the horizon and am shuffling, head down, inside my own little box constructed from "not fair," I find that I'm distracted by past and future "what ifs" and "shoulds." It's hard to feel thankful when it seems that everyone else is doing better, or there might not be enough for everyone, or that you've missed your opportunity, or that the scales of justice are somehow stacked against you. Simply reminding yourself that it's not a competition doesn't address the deeper sensation of separateness. This dualistic thinking, which is the thinking that keeps us locked out of gratitude, keeps us from seeing the unified oneness of everything. It keeps our lives, and our ability to give of ourselves, small. The trick is not to do more or buy more (strengthening the pull of competition), but to reconnect with the bigger picture, which is that the whole system is designed with you as an integral part and that each part influences the whole. Comparing ourselves to each other is like the foot being jealous of the hand; each part is essential in the working mobility of the human body. So it is with our role in human history and consciousness: each of us bringing something unique to the operation of the whole.

Practicing mindfulness combats the standard operating system of dualistic thinking. For me, walking is one of the quickest routes to recalibrate my connection to the whole. A walk outside softens me. It forces my mind and body to sync in the present moment. Mindfulness, simply bringing nonjudgmental attention to the present moment, can be done in meditation or throughout the day by bringing your awareness to whatever you're doing as you do it. Although mindfulness is a central theme in Buddhism, and as a practice has been around for centuries, as Macrina Wiederkehr says in *Seven Sacred Pauses*, it's "a universal quest and belongs to us all. Living mindfully is the art of living awake and ready to embrace the gift of the present moment." In fact, mindfulness practice is now widely embraced in public school classrooms and by CEOs. So, while developing a meditation practice is a formal form of cultivating mindfulness, there are many ways to strengthen this ability. Being in the moment, awake and aware of the gift of your life, is the process that lifts generosity out of the gratitude soup. Bringing your attention to something is mindfulness in action.

And as the French philosopher Simone Weil said, "Attention is the rarest and purest form of generosity." When we're paying attention, we're not only practicing gratitude for what is, but we're also being generous with our time, which is indeed our greatest asset. For me, there are days where my generosity is purely the attention I can give my children. When I set my phone to mute and get down on the floor to play, I give myself a chunk of time where I focus all my energy being in the moment with them. We play trains, or dinosaurs, or get into in-depth toddler discussions about whether Batman is stronger than Rainbow Dash. My four-year-old created a game called Storm where he runs through the house looking for a hiding place while I chase after him growling like thunder and flicking the lights on and off. This time spent with my boys is important generosity, and although it cannot be directly monetized it's just as valuable of a contribution of generosity as anything else I do in the community.

Our ability to hold this attention beyond our immediate loved ones allows us to witness an interconnectedness that is often fleeting but profoundly impactful when experienced. Tim Shriver, chairman of the Special Olympics, describes a moment like this where he is taken out of himself and moves into a unified field of oneness. "Many times I've watched, for instance, as a person with Down syndrome stands with a gold medal around her neck, arms raised high to a cheering crowd. I can't look at that child, at that human being, without slipping out of dualistic thinking. Those moments are a kind of sacrament of unitive consciousness. They are 'both-and' moments where shadow and light coexist in the same experience… Divine energy shoots vertically through me like a force, and says, 'See! Look! Pay attention to what is right in front of you! That is all you need to know!'" This practice of truly seeing others, and being with them where they are, strengthens our gratitude because it blurs the edges of where one ends and everything else begins. This oneness is always right in front of us if we pay attention, and this mindfulness expands our generosity as it lifts the veil of dualistic thinking.

In what way is your attention an act of generosity? Later in this section we'll add this to your giving plan.

Taking Care of Your Own Needs

Doing for others without first being *for and with* yourself creates resentment, and resentment is a major gratitude killer. We are only able to fully be in these moments, with focused time and attention, when we've done the work filling our own tanks first. Taking the time to nurture yourself is an investment in our collective experiential infrastructure—in fact, it's a matter of philanthropic practice. Just as financial advisors will tell you to put aside money for savings each month before you do anything else, I advise that you find ways to fill up your reserves before you attempt to give anything of yourself away. True joyful giving, the kind without strings attached, no barters, or trade-offs, is the kind of giving that fills others up. If you aren't first doing this for yourself, you won't be able to adequately do it for anyone else.

What are some of the ways you give to yourself? This might be as simple as getting eight hours of sleep each night and staying hydrated. I'm amazed at the difference simple biological needs play in maintaining my ability to be thankful and gracious. It might be creating some space for yourself that doesn't have a prescribed outcome. "Our being is often crowded out by our doing," says Macrina Wiederkehr, "Each day we are summoned to be creators of the present moment. Artists know the value of white space. Sometimes what isn't there enables us to see what is." Seeing what's really there is akin to paying attention; this time, directed toward yourself.

Clearing the deck of what you need to do in order to explore what feeds your energy grounds you within your philanthropic work, and if you are not aligned with your purpose (and can see clearly how your giving supports this purpose) it is more than easy to fall out of gratitude. It feels increasingly necessary in our connected world to follow the pings and alerts that tell us either that we're needed, or that we're missing opportunities, or that we're falling short. It's hard to find our reserves of generosity when we are constantly being pulled across time and space to attend to urgent matters. The lure of accomplishing tangible tasks puts off the importance of white space, yet it's this white space that enables us to accurately prioritize what matters. So much of this constant whir contributes to the vicious cycle of loneliness because we're busier than ever but we don't have the tools for intimacy and community. It all starts with you.

While this may seem like a luxury, to spend time in inquiry

about ourselves, it's a necessary practice for the joyful philanthropist. Spending time on yourself, and finding the ways you can connect with your passions in order to make the world a better place, is something we're all called to do. Without this personal inquiry, our actions come from an empty place, carrying the energy of "want" and "lack," which is detrimental for both the giver and receiver. This isn't the ego merely taking care of itself, prioritizing its own needs and wants over others; it is an urgent call to consider yourself the starting point for all the good that can happen on our planet. It is inquiry directed toward action. When you are not aligned, when the things you do are not in sync with what is important to you, you begin to feel taken advantage of. And you are the only gatekeeper for that.

Philanthropy is an everyday act, and to do this well we need to be clear with our boundaries and how much we can give. A joyful philanthropist is no more likely to give less of what she can than she will give more. Remember, *you can't give what you don't have.* In order to be generous with others, we must first be generous with ourselves. Ask yourself, *Am I taking care of myself? Am I meeting my own basic needs?* When I'm not generous with myself first, I don't have one generous bone to throw into the soup pot to feed the rest of my family, and certainly no one beyond them. You can only go so long giving on credit, both financially and emotionally. Setting up structures in your life that support experiences over stuff, while creating a mindfulness practice and honoring and nurturing your own needs, promotes philanthropic actions that are sustainable and full of joy.

Vulnerability as a Tool for Change

It's not enough to be thankful for the gifts we receive if we don't first understand our judgments and tackle our prejudices around the vulnerability of need. Possessing wealth or living in poverty are tangible concepts as they pertain to money, but they're intangible and existential when we consider what actually creates wealth or poverty in a life. We make ourselves vulnerable when we ask for help, and there is a cultural mindset that tells us that needing help means we're weak, or we're less than, or we weren't able to manage our life on our own. This is particularly sensitive in Western cultures where "pulling yourself up by your bootstraps" or "achieving the American dream" are lauded as heroine stories. Being vulnerable is not part of this mythology, and it makes us uncomfortable.

Yet vulnerability is the core of connection. It's the node in our network society. When you are able to shift your perception of those asking for help from "needy" to "grateful receiver," and acknowledge that you are also a grateful receiver, it becomes crystal clear that we are all in this dance together. Gratitude is a way of positioning ourselves in the world, like antennae intercepting radio waves, tuning into a frequency of gifts that are buzzing all around us: the food we eat, the house we live in, the plants that provide oxygen to breathe. We are recipients of gifts in every moment of every day. Acknowledging this creates a subtle shift in how we commonly understand giving and receiving as a linear transaction. The concepts of "wealthy" and "needy" are embedded in the either/or belief that one gives in order for the other to receive. In reality, it's circular.

The interchange of giving and receiving is beautiful when understood from this vantage point. You acknowledge that you're helping right now because you can, and you're helping right now because you know there will be a net to support you when it's your turn to ask. When we assume that those helping are better than those asking we have forgotten to see this pattern. We have forgotten that being able to give is a gift that strengthens our belief in humanity and our feelings of gratitude, and that this gift is only available to us because someone asked for help. It comes from a deep place of self-assuredness and humility to ask for help, and the best philanthropists are those who give with this same sense of vulnerability. Their giving says: *Thank YOU for letting me help, for seeing that I have something to give.*

From my experience working with nonprofits, foundations, and individual donors, I've come to appreciate the very real power structure in giving that was built from and replicates the status quo. At its best, philanthropy works against injustice and aims to support and sustain systemic change in our society. Yet often it falls short of this goal because it has become yet another player in the system. When you are a fish you don't realize you're swimming in water. Similar to the thought (often attributed to Albert Einstein) that we can't solve problems by using the same thinking we used when we created them, we can't promote justice using the same economic model that created the injustice.

This was Martin Luther King Jr.'s thought as well—that while philanthropy is admirable, "it must not cause the philanthropist to overlook the circumstances of economic injustice which make philanthropy necessary." I've encountered many good people who have been working at an entrenched problem for so long that they've lost track of the bigger conversation, and now are effectively working to support the system they're struggling against. And people mean well, but *feeling good* about our giving doesn't necessarily mean we're *doing good* with our giving. If we're so focused on solving a problem that we're avoiding the construct in which it first appeared, we're missing the opportunity to redefine the question. And when working on systemic injustices, it's important to ask questions that pull back the curtain and expose blind spots. These types of questions tend to make people uncomfortable because they expose vulnerabilities. It's important to ask anyway.

Here are a few for you to consider for yourself:

- How am I contributing to the problem of (homelessness) (gun violence) (climate change) (racial and gender inequity)? Is there a disconnect between how I'm living my life and what I then spend time and money trying to "fix"?
- In what ways do I, and the way I live my life, contribute to the circumstances of economic injustice that make philanthropy necessary in the first place? What would my philanthropy look like if I placed it at the front end of a system (at my own doorstep), rather than tackling the solution at the end of the problem?
- How can I construct a life that treads lightly and by its very nature makes things better from the start?
- How can I become a bit player, not the heroine, in someone else's story, enabling them to create their own impact? What if that person dislikes me and doesn't appreciate what I'm doing because they view me as part of the problem?

These are extremely personal questions, the answers to which might take a lifetime to contemplate as new scenarios push us further in our quest for authenticity. These questions tease at the assumption that things are supposed to be the way they are. *Are they?* How might a different set of assumptions change the way we construct our philanthropy? To maintain integrity in our philanthropic actions, it's essential to continually reexamine our beliefs. The inquiry and suggestions the authors provide in *Give Smart*, though developed to guide individuals with high net worth, pertain to all philanthropists who wish to tap into what matters in order to make a sustained difference. They place great emphasis on personal responsibility for the impact of donations, as well as reflect on the imbalance in the donor/grantee relationship. At one point they write: "How you approach your philanthropy offers the most unfiltered manifestation of who you really are as a human being. Generous or selfish. Wise or naïve. Humble or arrogant. Smart or impulsive. For better or worse, philanthropy is a defining act, one that can generate immense joy and a deep sense of personal fulfilment."

Giving and receiving with joy demands a high level of engagement and conscious effort to be clear of motives and desired outcomes. It takes diligence and concentrated effort to live a life of gratitude. It takes vulnerability to acknowledge and accept the gifts that others have for you and to give freely of yourself without feeling taken advantage of. Being aware of your intentions is a process that untangles your beliefs about money and resources and the ideas of wealth and want in your own life. This journey reminds us of our interconnectedness and brings the gift of deep purpose and joy. It also encourages simplicity.

CHAPTER NINE
Simplicity

"Live simply in order that others can simply live." —Ghandi

DEVELOPING GRATITUDE for *what is* cultivates a desire for simplicity. When you're focused on the present and appreciating that you already have everything you need, or that you can't change or control the circumstances and practice being thankful anyway, it becomes clear that the wanting and the striving is a distraction. The quiet space that emerges from gratitude amplifies what the heart wants, and what the heart wants is usually very simple. We clobber this internal voice with external noise because it's terrifying to consider all the implications of our lives; from acknowledging how our privilege impacts other people, countries, and the environment, to contemplating our time and the certainty of death. Being still enough to be overwhelmed by the utter heartbreaking beauty of life is a challenge that urges us to listen deeply to a voice we may not recognize. It's a lot easier to distract ourselves with sparkly things and fill our time with never ending to-do lists.

I ponder on simplicity and distraction a lot, wondering how we can recognize and appreciate what enough looks and feels like in our lives. How can we be better at community and connection? How do we combat the pull of more and return to that place of contentment over and over? What are we avoiding by keeping ourselves busy? Questioning how we fill our lives, our space and our time, is of ultimate importance as we develop our philanthropy. The questioning forces us to go deeper than any "how to simplify" list could ever provide. There are many books on the topic of living simply, from the "100 items challenge" to minimalist travel, from clutter-free guides to simplicity parenting. While all are valuable tools, they merely scratch the surface until you address the reasons for the distractions and meet the underlying fear head-on. Simplicity is your new way of eating rather than a thirty-day diet.

At its core, simplicity is a lifestyle that incorporates social justice and design. We create "good lives" by aligning our actions and our privilege with our values and philanthropic purposes, and this alignment streamlines our intent so the rest of the clutter falls away and the parts seamlessly merge with the whole. Simplicity is, as Leonardo da Vinci said, "the ultimate sophistication," for when you complete a full circle of this life contemplation you find yourself inside a complex wisdom. It is about nourishing your body and being present in your everyday interactions. It is also about having things around you that hold a story and serve a purpose—again, the concept of "right design"—which makes these items beautiful. This idea, to live simply so that others may simply live, is a mantra of the joyful philanthropist.

Having Enough and Letting Go

"The secret of happiness, you see, is not found in seeking more, but in developing the capacity to enjoy less." —Socrates

The adventure of simplicity is a journey to the heart of what matters, and unearthing purpose and connection. It is an opportunity to recognize your true giving potential, beyond dollar signs, to activate and align all actions in your life to create impact and joy. Developing your capacity to enjoy less begins with acknowledging what enough looks like in your life and letting go of everything else.

So, how much is enough? How much do you and your family need to live well? On the one hand, you can do some simple math and calculate how much money comes in and how much goes out. How much money comes in is usually set by external forces: the pay scale for your chosen career, or the loss of a job. But where your money goes can bring up uncomfortable questions about waste and privilege. It certainly has for me. I've begun to look around my house and see my material items as "food for a family," and "an education for a young woman." It's not just how much money I make that allows me to be a philanthropist, it's also the choices I make in how to spend that money.

Yet there doesn't need to be as much discrepancy as there is. The core of "enough" is an experience rather than a place to arrive: it's wanting what we have, rather than having whatever we want. This experience of having and wanting shouldn't vary depending on how much money you have. The essential elements of living a good life are based on survival and beauty, the ideal being that you are comfortable and enjoying the things around you. This might scale up or down with more or less money, but even those with great financial reserves can be uncomfortable and not enjoying what's around them. Those with less might actually have a lot less existential worry and obligations to fulfill. What we're talking about here isn't merely economic. Every one of us has the ability to live a life of enough, to find our right livelihood and experience wealth.

We've gotten stuck in a singular definition of wealth as being an abundance of something of monetary value that is worthy of exchange. Yet wealth comes in a plethora of forms, from a wealth of friendships to a wealth of time. A redefinition would be *an abundance of anything of beauty in our lives that brings us health and happiness*. I consider my assets to include my kind and generous neighbors, the time I get to spend with my kids, and the giant madrone tree in my front yard. These would never make it onto a spreadsheet of actual assets, because how do you place value on the intangible? Does this make them any less valuable? What accounting do we hold so holy that it wouldn't include these very important, and very necessary, elements of individual wealth?

"The cultivation and expansion of needs," E.F. Schumacher posits in *Small is Beautiful: Economics as if People Mattered*, "is the antithesis of wisdom. It is also the antithesis of freedom and peace. Every increase of needs tends to increase one's dependence on outside forces over which one cannot have control, and therefore increases existential fear. Only by a reduction of needs can one promote a genuine reduction in those tensions which are the ultimate causes of strife and war." Drawing a direct correlation between our increase in needs and the fear and strife manifesting in the world points out the role each individual plays in the system. It can't be underestimated the power that each of us possesses. Every day presents us with an opportunity to make a choice for freedom and peace. How do we do this?

There are many people and organizations pondering what a restructured economy might look like. From Bioneers, an educational organization that promotes nature and community as our greatest resource to restoring earth, to Community Supported Agriculture (CSA), which uses a cooperative model to allow individuals to buy locally produced food directly from the producers. There is talk of a sharing economy, a regenerative economy, a gifting economy. Businesses and nonprofits are blurring the lines of giving back when they focus on social investments and triple bottom lines. Community Sourced

Capital, located in Seattle, created a business offering loans gathered from individuals in the form of "squares" to small, local businesses. This idea is similar to many investment groups around the country, like LION in Port Townsend, Washington, who use money from local individuals to build prosperous local businesses, keeping investment money in their community, and helping build a more resilient and sustainable economy in their town. There are also TimeBanks, where you can input your skills and offer out your availability in order to gain help in another area, based on how much of your own time you've "spent." These models are all based on a relationship economy, one in which we focus on bringing together the giver and receiver in a holistic transaction that creates benefits where the whole is greater than the sum of its parts. Sharing, regenerative, gifting…the real economy is about relationship.

When I left my job to stay home with our son, I had an experience at my bank that highlighted the great lack of imagination we've employed in creating and sustaining our current economy. I was meeting with a young banker to discuss the penalty fees assessed to my account for no longer having a direct monthly deposit. I explained that I would be freelancing and would like to maintain some kind of account to deposit payments. He couldn't understand why I would need my own bank account if I didn't have a job (with a direct deposit), and a husband with an account that I could deposit my money into. Round and round we went (with some women's history thrown in) until I gave up and withdrew the remaining funds. In that moment, a twenty-plus-year relationship was severed and I was embarrassed and angry. I had been rendered invisible within a system I had become dependent on.

That experience, though minor and merely hurtful as opposed to damaging my chances of survival, gave me insight into the reality of many others. There are currently large multinational banks charging $12 a month for checking accounts unless you have an account balance of $1,500 or a monthly direct deposit of at least $250. While I did have other financial options, I could recognize the injustice and how the game was rigged. And beyond that, I contemplated the message behind the policy: if my time is no longer worth money, and my money is no longer worth someone else's time, where is my life force in this equation? Where is my value? For that matter, what worth do children have? Do retirees? Or any of those working for minimum wage? Our economic system currently doesn't have the ability to reflect the myriad ways humans provide value in their communities. It is also rife with predatory lending practices and racism and contributes to the cycle of poverty. Further, it cultivates want and encourages a feedback loop that expands to greater and greater depths. We are under pressure to live within this status quo and many of us have forgotten that we are part of, not separate from, nature's economy. We've reduced life to an economic equation, placing dollar signs over our heads, and if things (or people) do not establish economic value, there is no way to place value on them at all. We created this. And we can change it.

The complication in changing this system comes when you begin evaluating what lifestyle you want. It's a simple calculation to determine the amount of money you need to support "having enough." But what lifestyle do you deem appropriate in comparison to those around you with less, which doesn't adversely impact the environment? I was having a discussion with girlfriends about what we could do with a windfall of money if one of us won the lottery. We worked out the finances, considered taking the lump sum versus annual payouts. We talked about the big splurges we might make, the gifts and support we could give to family members. This was the simple calculation of numbers in and numbers out, deciding how much we'd need to take care of ourselves and our families.

But then the talk turned to managing the relationship dynamics of having more than others. We talked about jealousy from friends and entitlement of children. We thought about the space we'd be creating between ourselves and the rest of the world. We wondered how we could keep the money secret and continue to live primarily as we do now. Because we knew that just because we *can* have something, doesn't mean we should, and our new wealth wouldn't serve the greater good if it was only serving us. Ultimately, we agreed we'd need to set up a system to give most of it away. After bills were paid and loved ones were taken care of, there wasn't really much more we wanted. We realized we'd be happiest using the money to support and do work that benefited others. Which brought me back to this book, and the belief that we could all be doing this work of strategizing resources in order to better serve the greater good, regardless of how much money we have. Money is great at taking care of basic needs, but beyond that, it fills an ever widening hole of want that could be filled in better ways.

Living simply is an ongoing conversation with the world around you. Mistakes are lessons and the striving is circular: we are relearning how to live in relationship. There is a groundswell of energy around simplifying our material possessions, living a tad smaller, and being more present in our communities. The drive for bigger and better has led many Americans to a dead end, or more aptly, to a spiral of want that has no end. Many of us are opting out, searching for ways to minimize our footprint and spend more time *with* each other than *on* each other.

Ask yourself the following questions and listen for the quiet voice that calls forth a world in which we are more connected and resources are distributed equitably.

- What is the most cherished gift you've given to someone?
- What is the most cherished gift you've received?

- If you had everything you needed, what would you give? To whom, and in order to do what?

In the 1971 film *Harold and Maude*, one of my all-time favorite movies, there's a scene where Harold gives Maude a ring and professes his love for her. She thanks him and promptly throws it into the water so she'll always know where to find it. Of course Harold is taken aback, disappointed that she threw his gift away, but Maude has received his sentiment and is free of the burden of the object. We learn that Maude was a survivor of the Holocaust and her appreciation for life came from her early relationship with death. The perspective she holds is that wanting things is a direct cause of fear and war, and she can be an active participant in creating freedom and peace by simply letting go.

Want and desire are elements of the human condition that lead to jealousy and envy, not to mention family rivalry, world wars, and individual depression. This was painfully illustrated for me several years ago when I traveled back to Montana to spend Memorial Day weekend with my ninety-year-old grandparents. The whole family went back, a planned visit when we could all be there, in order to go through their house and divvy up "stuff" in preparation for their move to an assisted-living facility. Problem was, Grandfather was in early-stage dementia and had forgotten he'd planned this weekend, so we arrived like vultures picking meat off of the bones of a still-living animal. He became sullen and angry; my mother got into an argument with her mother that ended with both of them in tears and my grandmother storming into her room and locking her door. Meanwhile, the rest of us got into the scotch and watched my son ride a cane around the house like a wooden horsey.

Divvying up the stuff in my grandparents' house became more competition between siblings, more proof of favoritism, more fodder for hurt feelings. There's this little voice inside saying, "I want it I want it I want it," which sounds childish and feels wronged. I experienced it while I was there. I could feel the pull of the undercurrent, taunting me that I wasn't going to get anything if I didn't speak up. I took some time to walk through the house looking at everything with the eyes of wanting and I could see a few things that I wouldn't mind having. But I also felt the deep pain of a losing game: as soon as I became invested in wanting something, I was setting myself up to be hurt by not getting it.

I made the walk through their house a meditation, placing my hands on items, looking deeply at them and remembering the feelings and the stories surrounding them. I have them in my heart. Like Maude, I too would like to throw my most prized possessions into the middle of a lake. To know that things can remain meaningful in my mind and heart, even if they're not in my hand. I hope to remember as I age to begin parting with cherished items as I go: to children and grandchildren, my jewelry, my plates, and to friends and neighbors, shoes that don't fit, handbags no longer necessary. Let me remember not to place too much importance on the material item. I started repeating in my head, "I have everything I need already. I am so lucky. I have everything I need *and more* already."

Much easier in theory than practice, but practice is all there is. And practice will help. After these visits with my grandparents I become absorbed with thoughts of how to age gracefully; how to let go of the things I could once do, the things I once had, while watching the younger ones soar into the height of their energy and success. How do I cultivate joy in passing the baton to the next generation? Because having enough isn't just about the tangible stuff of life, it's also an exercise in letting go of all the things you don't or can't have. It's letting go of having anything except for what you already have, and rejoicing in those things. And this is contrary to how, at least in the West, we've been indoctrinated. We've been raised assuming we'll do better than our parents, that we should have more than our neighbors, that we can aspire to be rich and famous—that this can all happen in our lifetime because we live in a time of affluence. Anything we want can be conjured. A click of the button on a whim brings deliveries to your door within a day.

But should it? Just because we can, doesn't mean we should.

I also find that as I give things away that I no longer need or that no longer add value, I have a feeling of wealth. The space that is left adds lightness and opens up opportunities for other types of things to enter. In letting go of something I acknowledge that I have something to give, therefore I possess a wealth of something. A wealth of canning jars, perhaps, a wealth of shoes…things that I do not need multiples of that someone else is happy to receive. I feel this in reverse as well, when someone gives me something right at the moment that I need it. A new *to me* summer dress is a pick-me-up that provides me with a feeling of wealth and encourages me to move something else along that's been taking up space in my cabinets. The act of listening to what others need or want and happening upon that thing in your home that you no longer need or want is a gift to both parties. You are participating in the dance of giving and receiving, and when you're in that space you can feel time slow down. The ability to be in the present moment hinges on the balance of listening and acting. You enter the flow, that creative moment when you are immersed in an activity for its own sake and time disappears—you forget yourself and feel a part of something larger.

There is a cool social movement taking place across the country called the Buy Nothing Project, which "offer(s) people a way to give and receive, share, lend, and express gratitude through a worldwide network of hyper-local gift economies in which the true wealth is the web of connections formed between people who are real-life neighbors." Started on Bainbridge Island, Washington, in 2013 by Liesl Clark and Rebecca Rockefeller, they've grown to over 800 groups worldwide, encouraging community around the world by providing a platform for neighbors to give each other things they no longer need. Rather than take things to the dump or Goodwill, or head to the store to buy something new, you can extend the life cycle of an object and create community through a simple transaction. One of my favorite principles of the Buy Nothing Project is: "We are a gift economy, not a charity. We see no difference between want and need, waste and treasure." Recognizing that we all have something to give and we all are in need of something, Buy Nothing is an important aspect of feminist philanthropy because it blurs the lines between giving and receiving, creating something entirely new, bestowing a simple transaction with the power to transform a community.

Similar to Marion Rockefeller Weber's "flow funding," the dance of giving and receiving allows money and stuff and time to flow spontaneously to the exact place it is needed. While Weber's flow funding specifically engages social innovators and visionaries to make grants, her democratic idea of philanthropy urges all of us to get involved, with whatever we have available to give. We are all experts in our neighborhoods and within our personal relationships, and we have everything we need, right now, to make a difference. But we can't make a difference if we hold on to what we have; we have to let it go. Practicing joyful philanthropy is a way of remembering that life is fleeting and what we acquire, gather, and accumulate will stay here after we've gone. Letting our time and money and everything embodied within these elements flow through us, rather than stick with us, is a clear pathway to experiencing joy.

One of the most impactful moments in my life came when I let go of The Ruby Room and allowed it to flow through, and beyond, me. When my cofounder and I started the organization over a decade ago, I was certain I knew the direction it should take. I was deeply invested in the outcome and worked day and night to get the mission established and successful. But right from the start the idea of providing prom dresses to high school girls took on a life of its own. I remember telling people the idea felt like a train that was leaving the station and I had to decide whether to climb aboard. This thing was moving. I learned and relearned this lesson during those early startup days: this thing I was creating didn't belong to me, I was merely the conduit for it to come into existence.

Seven years after I'd resigned from the board of directors, I had another opportunity to revisit this lesson. I was attending the annual Ruby Room fundraiser and when I walked into the Campion Ballroom on the Seattle University campus, I did not recognize a single person there. What's more, *no one recognized me*. It was an odd sensation to look around at a room full of people, spending money and supporting an idea that I'd launched, and realize that, to them, I was just another guest. I had taken an idea, watched it grow and evolve, and then grow beyond my scope. Those first years spent developing a brand, being interviewed by local media, building a board, establishing a budget and relationships with donors, and housing hundreds of prom dresses in my 500-square-foot studio, felt very much a part of my identity; but, of course, it was very much a separate entity that existed outside of me. The little idea of providing prom dresses was embraced by hundreds of people outside my zone of influence, and the day-to-day workings were continuing on after I had left. It was a thrilling feeling, and a pivotal moment in my life. It is all too easy to become attached to the things we create, to want recognition and praise for the ideas we have and promote. But it is joyful to release expectations of ownership and outcome, to let ideas and relationships and stuff flow through.

Letting go is constantly underway around us. The seasons gracefully make way for each other to emerge, year in and year out. The waxing and waning of the moon, the waves approaching and retreating from the shore. Our own breath, coming in and out…these are all reminders that by letting go, we receive. So while the universe presents us with a multitude of opportunities to practice letting go, sometimes we need something more concrete. Here are two ways to bring this practice into your life that will provide you with immediate feedback:

First, an easy way to make letting go a daily or weekly practice is to tuck a box in a closet or corner of your house and begin to fill it with stuff you don't need. I always have one going on top of the washing machine. I'm baffled at how easy it is for stuff to come into the house and get "stuck" somewhere. Rather than doing a giant purge each spring, I casually grab things as I walk by them and put them in the box all year long. When the box gets full I take a few moments to pull the things I can post on Buy Nothing, consider what can go into an annual garage sale, and the rest gets dropped off at a Goodwill truck. I'm constantly floored at how often the box fills up. And I can say with certainty, I've never missed anything after it's gone.

This exercise is more challenging to do with young children, as the world wants to give them stuff to bring home all the time, and my attempts to let their stuff "flow through" is often met with great angst. Children shine a light on our basest desires to keep things, and our delight over something "new." This feeling of not having enough and wanting more is universal. As my boys get older I'm working on ways to encourage them to implement a similar practice of passing things along. Rather than boxing their stuff up when they're out of the house, I'm looking for ways to talk with them about the practice and stoke their personal desire to let go. I've found that what truly helps is if they have someone specific to give to. It feels better to give something we once loved or valued to someone who will appreciate it, rather than anonymously dropping it off at a collection site. You think of a person, whether you know them personally or not, who needs this item and will find enjoyment from it and it becomes easier to part with it. The item itself becomes a meaningful connection, and the giving away carries a feeling of joy.

Second, building off of the time schedule in Section Two, write down three things you want desperately to do. For example, you want to meditate, play soccer, and refinish the cabinets. Out of your list of three things, commit to making one of them happen (start with just one!); then look for the thing that is holding you back, and let that thing go. For example, in order to meditate you need to turn off the TV earlier in the evening. In order to play soccer on the weekends you need to drop your book club. If you're going to refinish the cabinets you need to let the laundry pile up a bit while you attend to the project. Time is finite. We say we don't have time for something, and this is true. You can't keep adding activities without deprioritizing others. We keep ourselves busy in order to drown out the deepest desires of the heart. Yet it is when we allow ourselves to experience the things we truly, desperately want, that the need for busyness and addiction to acquiring stuff greatly loosens its hold. And if you aren't ready to leave the book club, soccer will have to wait. You might come to realize you like the idea of soccer, but aren't actually that interested. Recognizing the trade-off makes the decision more intentional, and makes it easier to immerse yourself more fully into what you *are* doing. Every decision is a choice, but perhaps more importantly, every nondecision is also a choice. By not choosing something you are making a very clear decision. Own it.

Establishing Your Giving Potential

"Earth provides enough to satisfy every (wo)man's need, but not for every (wo)man's greed." —Gandhi

Joyful philanthropists have determined how much is enough for them to live well and embraced the flow of letting go. This practice allows them to then begin identifying how much is possible for them to give. The last bit of Nordhoff's quote, that a philanthropist is determined by a generous heart *giving as much as possible*, is a call to action to establish our giving potential. How much you are able to give is the outcome of how much you have minus how much you need. It is also determined by your ability to nurture and strengthen your generous heart. The idea of your personal giving potential is a profound concept because the answer to "what is possible" is going to be unique for everyone; giving as much as possible is an ongoing balance and redistribution. It isn't giving more than you have, and it's acknowledging where you could give more.

Your giving potential is also aspirational, providing something to work toward. According to the Urban Institute, most households in the United States give between 2–5% of income, so you might decide your ideal giving would fall in that range. But this is just one slice of your philanthropy, and using the work from this book, you'll also want to consider all of your other resources for giving. Perhaps you're in a financial position that allows you to give a couple hundred dollars a year, but you can commit 10% of your time. Or you give 3% financially, and match that with another 3% of your time and skills to support the same work. Maybe you decide to stretch yourself year over year, making lifestyle changes that propel you toward an annual gift of 10% that is a combination of money, time, and skills. Write down your giving goals and work backward to figure out how to make these calculations a reality.

These giving goals might also evolve and change through the years because what's possible for you today might not be tomorrow. The resources you have available to give this year might change next year as you're called to take care of sick child or parent, or you're given a promotion that adds monetary means but takes away some of your available time. If you get clear on all the moving pieces that contribute to your giving potential, you can allow it to flex throughout your life, while remaining rooted in what's possible right now.

Be curious, rather than judgmental, when you wonder about possibility in your philanthropy. Ask yourself, *How much* is *possible?*

The work of answering this question starts with addressing some deeply held beliefs about things like homeownership, retirement, and family commitments, while tackling a few untruths that our society tells us: that it's us versus them, there are haves and have-nots and that there's not enough to go around. Not to mention the deception that we live in an equitable system that treats everyone fairly if they try hard enough—that it's a personal choice how much money we have and that the system isn't actually engineered to maintain the status quo, elevating some while devaluing others. The question of how much is possible is immense and inky because you're not only calling into question how much money you have and how much money you need, and where and how to spend your time, you're questioning everything you have and need in life. You're questioning whether you're spending your life on the right things. This inquiry invites you to step outside of the current social construct and look back in at yourself to see if it's a good fit for you.

Follow the rabbit hole, and asking how much you need to live well morphs into yet a deeper question: What does it *mean* to live well? We need to eat. Somewhere to sleep. Something to do that makes us feel competent and creative. People to love, who love us back. *Everything else is extra.* Consider that almost half the world's population, over three billion people, live on less than $2.50 a day. More than 1 billion people have inadequate access to clean water and 2.6 billion lack basic sanitation. According to an article on GlobalIssues.org, in the US we spend $8 billion on cosmetics while only $6 billion is spent on basic education in developing countries. And the website *Giving What You Can* states that if you earn more than $50,000 per year (in a single adult household), you are in the richest 1.3% of the world's population; even a family of four at $50,000 per year has an income which is thirteen times the global average. According to the 2014 Census ACS survey, the median household income for the United States was $53,657.

However, a more recent study published on CNN Money shows that almost half of all American families (51 million households) can't afford basics like food and rent. So even when unemployment is low, people are still struggling. Which means there are other factors to consider, like wages and cost of living, and an economic system that supports and perpetuates racial and gender inequity. If you are part of the 50% of Americans thriving in this system, what is your responsibility in helping the other half? Being informed about where you find yourself in this data provides a picture of the needs of others compared to your own, and gives you the tools to make decisions about your giving potential.

Now, let me be clear. If you are thriving in this system, it is a call to action to acknowledge the struggles of others and get real about your privilege. My intent is not to guilt people or shame them for the life they've built, however, it's important to hold up a mirror and reflect on our stories of struggle and success in order to expand our generosity. This is particularly true in the Pacific Northwest bubble where I live. It's easy to go through a day, or maybe several weeks, without seeing the reality of struggle and suffering that so many face. Certainly there are clues to the level of need, like the homeless encampments that have expanded across the city. But in general, without being informed of the facts and wondering about causes, it's easy to get trapped in the idea that most people are doing okay.

So while anything is possible, *how much is possible* is entirely up to you. It starts with a choice that you want to make it possible. Developing your giving potential is a personal journey of coming back to the present moment, over and over, finding contentment with what you have and what you're able to give. The full potential of which is determined first by your commitment to create the world you want to live in. Your passion, outlined in previous pages, will drive and sustain you as you enter the following conversation, where we start putting all the pieces together and contemplate what it means to live "a good life." Knowing what you're passionate about softens the edges around the discussions on legacy, giving things away, and finding your personal place of "enough." Committing to your passion gives you the stamina to determine how much is possible to live a good life while helping others. And you might be surprised what you are able to give as the muscles of generosity, compassion, and joy have been reinforced.

Finally, developing your giving potential is personal, but it shouldn't be private. Changing the world is political. It demands that we talk with each other about it. Don't keep your giving private—talk about what you're doing, how you're involved, and the sacrifices you're making in order to create meaningful change in your community. A large part of joyful philanthropy is encouraging others to play too. You have the power to influence others around you by speaking your truth about why and how and where you give of yourself. Being a philanthropist today means being an everyday changemaker;

someone who is giving as much as possible to sustain and support their passion. Start wherever you are, and reflect on what *giving as much as possible* means to you.

CHAPTER TEN
The Map: Your Giving Plan

YOUR GIVING plan is where you put all this information into a simple document that you can easily refer to and update. Gathering all of your thoughts together is necessary to create a template for action. It's a living document, and as such, it can and should change and evolve over the years. You'll be able to make notes and build on previous years so that you can better understand your impact. It's a tool, much like a roadmap.

You're pinning the existential ideas of giving into a fabric of reality. Because it's all well and good to talk about systems design and the web of life, but what will you say when your neighbor asks for a sponsorship for her 5k run in support of Parkinson's? How will you respond when your extended family insists on maintaining the tradition of giving everyone a gift on Christmas morning? Framing your passions and intent into a strategic plan helps define the gray areas. You can throw these requests up against the giving plan you've created and see what sticks and what doesn't. Viewing singular requests as part of a larger philanthropic goal provides you with the reasoning why you can't give in certain situations and why others resonate so strongly.

A giving plan is more than a financial document. A giving plan includes every resource you possess, the sum total of your giving, in order to make the world a better place. If you've done the previous work to narrow your passions and get focused, this doesn't have to be as broad and diluted as it sounds. Your focus enables you to expand your ability to give. Think about a prism: a single shaft of light comes in and is then focused to a point where it is able to explode onto the wall in a dazzling display of rainbow. So too is your giving. Your personal light, narrowed and focused, finds a path to expand out in an array of giving far beyond an undiluted outpouring alone. This plan is your prism.

So while there are spots to include your financial giving, there are also places to include your time, attention, networks, skills, and stuff. These are all your resources to give. The concept of the prism also illuminates the other side of the giving coin: how we make a life. Rather than drawing arbitrary lines between the money we spend to "do good" and the money we spend to "make a life," we can look for the places where our spending, donating, and investing can intersect. We don't all have the capacity to make large charitable donations, but we do spend money. And where this money is spent, how it flows into and out of our lives, is the crux of being an informed philanthropist, someone who cares about humanity and uses her resources intentionally.

When you want your resources, *all of your resources*, to help nurture and sustain your community, it becomes clear that philanthropy goes beyond a traditional financial donation. Your time, skills, and money become valued resources that manifest from your core, applied liberally throughout your day. Would you consider a financial investment in a local business part of your philanthropy? Do you think of yourself as a philanthropist when you support an emerging artist by buying a piece of her art? Or when you volunteer at a neighborhood school? Further, would paying reparations to the people and places you benefit from, like the Duwamish Tribe's Real Rent effort, be a part of your annual giving? There are a multitude of creative ways your time, money, and skills can be given, and with knowledge and intention they contribute to a strategic and joyful philanthropic plan. This is living your philanthropy—it puts "being" at the heart of your "doing." It's an intentional acknowledgment that *how* we give and receive is the true currency with which to create lasting change.

Download a template giving plan on my website at www.kristencorningbedford.com/worksheets

FOUR | PUTTING IT ALL TOGETHER

"The map is not the territory."

—Alfred Korzybski

All of these pieces of information you've been gathering, about your external and internal worlds and your place in them, have led you here to this moment. You have created a foundation for giving and strategies to do it well. You have been encouraged to think more systemically, imagining the scenario upstream. You are curious about alternate ways of knowing and emboldened to question the status quo. You have explored how receiving gifts from others is integral in the flow of giving, and hopefully have a better appreciation for doing so with joy. And you've created your giving plan, with clear intentions and directions for action.

It feels like a culmination, but in fact it's just the beginning...as Pope Francis so pointedly stated: "Our goal is not to amass information or to satisfy curiosity, but rather to become painfully aware, to dare to turn what is happening to the world into our own personal suffering and thus to discover what each of us can do about it." For me, this is when I realize how much more work I have to do. To take all of this information in and allow it to become a part of me. The exploration of philanthropy begins to alter us on a molecular level. Like a piece of clay in a kiln, our structure begins to change in order for our core to become more resilient and durable. Through this transformation we find ourselves less fragile, and our ability to give becomes sustainable. It is a process, and it takes time and care. In order to do the work that must be done, we need to sink deeply into our desires for a better world, for everyone, and come back from the kiln ready to serve.

Your giving plan is a map, not the territory. The document you've created, while necessary, will not give you the relationships and perspective needed to be an effective philanthropist. In order to be effective in seeking and promoting the welfare of others, you must also be willing to be vulnerable, to be wrong, and to be open to change. Examining questions about your privilege and applying generosity in ways that feel foreign and uncomfortable create new ways to cultivate your philanthropy. Once you've embraced the idea that philanthropy is not something that lives as an activity outside of you, but is a core tenet of who you are, the door opens to a more nuanced understanding of it. One that does not allow you to come in at the end and solve other people's problems. One that forces you to accept your role in the social, environmental, and economic inequity that makes philanthropy necessary. This philanthropy is based in fixing *that* problem.

By using our unique lens to interpret what we see and feel, we pull up the floorboards on the way things are. The ability to direct our resources, shaped by a personal giving strategy, becomes a political act that can shift our current cultural climate. Tapping into our deepest desires opens the possibility that there is another way—to live, to create, to be in relationship with the world around us. The future is dependent on shifting our group identities to become more inclusive and building something new with the floorboards.

CHAPTER ELEVEN
The Territory: Expanding the Limits of Generosity

THE ROAD to hell, they say, is paved with good intentions, and this might be most true when applied to philanthropy. While generosity is the linchpin of giving, it isn't enough to be generous if you aren't questioning the circumstances that provided you with the resources to give and the need for giving in the first place. Without this personal inquiry your generosity is an exercise in self-congratulation, barely scratching the surface of inequity. In fact, it might be further contributing to the inequalities you are proudly trying to eradicate. Because the truth is, if your intent is justice, your actions will look very different from helping to solve the problem. You would be questioning the systems that created them.

From this line of questioning you begin to see a new map being drawn, one that demands a different kind of action. This new map will show us roads we haven't seen before: to get to *giving as much as possible* we have to not take as much; to get to *helping others* we have to recognize ourselves as other; to get to *generosity* we have to work for justice. These roads are right in front of us, yet elusive. Because creating lasting, systemic change is about building bridges to new systems from the old ones, and in order to do this we have to first be able to see the old systems for what they are. We have to understand the role we play in this old system and shake free of the privilege this placement affords us. Only then can we begin to build out new ways of thinking, which, combined with humility and sacrifice, is where we'll begin to see a shift.

Not Taking as Much in Order to Give as Much as Possible: What Is Your Good Life?

Asking yourself how much is too much to take really starts with the question: *What is a good life?* We are taught by society and advertising and models of success what *the* good life looks like: jet-setting vacations, toned bodies, maybe a house by the sea and a fast car. Striving for *the* good life is the antithesis to not taking as much. It is a vision for more, and is detached from reality for the vast majority of us. There is a subtle, but important, distinction between having *the* good life and having *a* good life. Using the word *the* creates comparison and competition because it purports to say there's only one path for a good life. In living *the* good life there is always an undercurrent of wanting. Living *a* good life is *your* good life. This life is utterly up to your discretion and is not dependent on what others think. The definition varies from "a life abounding in material comforts and luxuries" to "a life lived according to the moral and religious laws of one's culture." Individuals tend to offer up components that fall along this spectrum: health, family, enough money to cover necessities, a sense of purpose. Living *a* good life is a philosophical proposition: you are living a good life when you stop wanting a better one.

What would it take to be satisfied with what you have right now? Somewhere in the space between what you can acquire and what difference you hope to make is that place called *enough*. There is a lot of talk of abundance and scarcity when discussing our ability to give, but I now prefer to root the conversation in the concept of "enough," as Vicki Robin suggests in *Your Money or Your Life*. For years I've considered the abundance in my life when discussing the ways in which I give back: where do I give because I have too much, and where do I retreat in order to protect my own livelihood. But I've come to realize that abundant may not be the right model to embrace and aspire to. Abundance looks like a windfall or the land of plenty. Abundant feels like "more"; it is ever expanding. Whenever we reach *more*, we find there could still be more. What we need to settle into is the feeling of satiety. You develop your potential for giving by knowing how much is enough for you to live a good life while still having something available to help others. The two foundational components to any philanthropic plan are, first, understanding and appreciating what your good life looks like, and second, acknowledging that everyone has the right to some version of this good life. Taken a step further, it's recognizing that these two components are not mutually exclusive.

This thinking has provided a pivotal shift in how I approach simplicity and giving back to my community. And I'm not ashamed to admit that it's taken me to a place rich with contradiction. I know how to talk the talk, but I'm still built within the context of my environment, my place in time and my privilege. I come from a long line of explorers and entrepreneurs; people who strove to make it to the edge and carve out an existence in new territory. Many of us in the Western world have this history embedded in our DNA. We are born of the frontier, and it feels like there is always something better over the next hill. Those hills are now metaphorical: a new car, a second helping, another volunteer commitment. We fill our lives and our time with things beyond our capacity or need. And it's not a stretch to understand that in these moments we have stepped outside of the balanced reciprocity of giving and receiving and entered a time of taking and extracting. I have a long way to go before I'm truly living within my means: not the budget for my household, but humanity's careful balance of the world's available resources, spanning generations into the future.

And yet, I'm coming around to wanting to live smaller. I have visions of the new great horizon facing humanity and it's not pretty. As Annie Leonard, executive director of Greenpeace USA and the filmmaker behind *The Story of Stuff*, asked, "Are we going to change by design or by default?" I'd rather make a conscious design decision to live within my means while providing for others around me than have this decision forced upon me by external environmental forces. It may already be too late for my efforts to make an impact worldwide, but perhaps they'd make an impact within my direct circle of influence. And maybe that's enough. Maybe that's all it would take. So, I choose to trudge along, course correcting as best I can and voraciously practicing how to better walk the talk. I choose to be part of the design team by putting my philanthropy at the center of my simplified life. Because we have a choice to move through life as creators or consumers, and the future is dependent on creators.

The piece you ultimately can control is creating a good life. I think it's important to pause here and ask you to consider what *your* good life looks like. Get specific—whether it's sitting at the beach reading a book or leading a board meeting, write down what a good life means to you. Get lost in the imagery of this good life and write up how it makes you feel to be living it. The Harvard Study of Adult Development, a research project spanning seventy-five years and cataloging the lives of 724 men, has formulated a clear takeaway on what makes a good life. In his November 2015 TEDx Talk, Robert Waldinger explained that social connections and good relationships make us happier and healthier. There is a direct correlation between the quality of our relationships and the health of our brains. As Mark Twain said, "the good life is built with good relationships." (and with all due respect to Twain, I think he meant to say *a* good life.) Atul Gawande, the author of *Being Mortal*, believes that people feel their life is good as long as they have the continued ability to be charting the course of their own lives. So what about you? What makes your life good? Sometimes it's easier to think about in smaller increments, so maybe ask yourself: What makes a good day?

Reflecting on the nature of our impermanence is the surest way to distill this. Watching a neighbor clear out his childhood home after his mother passes away, or a friend fight cancer so she'll be able to watch her young sons grow up. In these moments you find yourself precariously in the center of the fast-moving stream of humanity, and it becomes painfully clear how quickly life passes and how the simple things have the most impact. Gawande beautifully captures this in his book, when he defines death as the gift that gives perspective to our life. "As our time winds down, we all seek comfort in simple pleasures—companionship, everyday routines, the taste of good food, the warmth of sunlight on our faces. We become less interested in the rewards of achieving and accumulating, and more interested in the rewards of simply being. Yet while we may feel less ambitious, we also become concerned for our legacy. And we have a deep need to identify purposes outside ourselves that make living feel meaningful and worthwhile." Death is our gentle reminder to not take as much; to instead focus on being present and thankful.

There's a further reckoning here, outlined succinctly in Richard V. Reeves's book *Dream Hoarders*. In his book he explains that while we're all focused on the top 1%, the most consequential income gap is happening between the upper middle class—those in the top 20%—and everyone else. He states that half of the people making more than $100,000 a year think you need at least $500,000 a year to count as "rich"; however, with the spread between incomes, those of us who thought we were middle class are actually the new upper middle to upper class. And we're hoarding the opportunities that provide our children with the ability to stay in this income bracket by using the benefits of living with privilege. Donating back to society with one hand, while contributing to the problem with the other, maintains the status quo while we pat ourselves on the back for doing something good. Giving our time and money shouldn't negate the need to make choices in our lifestyles that support a good life for others. Affluent parents might not purposefully be doing anything wrong by working hard and providing opportunities for their kids. Making a phone call to a friend to help your son get an internship or buying a house in a neighborhood with a good school seem innocuous actions on their own, but Reeves points out that cumulatively, they are privileges that keep some families rising up the ladder of prosperity while actively holding others down.

Part of the responsibility of a philanthropist is taking a hard look at how we're living our lives and the benefits we receive from the opportunities we've been given, while becoming informed about how these benefits arose from a system of inequity. It's taking responsibility for that privilege by deciding to live more simply so that others can have access to similar opportunities. It's letting go of the idea that we can (or should) elevate our children's success over others'. Reeves ends his book with the following request: "My hope, and belief, is that those of us in the upper middle class are willing to risk a fraction of our home values by rezoning our neighborhoods in favor of some higher density housing; willing to lose exclusivity in the kind of kids our own go to school with; willing to marginally lessen their chances of landing a plum college place as we agree to eradicate legacy preferences; willing to accept a slightly harder transition to the labor market by democratizing internships; and willing to pay a bit more tax to fund more opportunities for children less fortunate than our own."

Awakening to the ways our lifestyles are directly contributing to inequity in our communities and the degradation of our environment is a major step in recognizing that we have enough, and perhaps more than enough. A good life is built from this foundation and will change the way you see your role in making a lasting difference. Your privilege, if used correctly, becomes a gift that can transform the narrative and create action at a level not currently accessible to others. The only way to activate this gift, however, is to allow yourself to become a bit uncomfortable and then sacrifice some of your own self-interest in the short term. The long view gives new perspective on the infinite possibilities of a good life for all.

Victoria Woodhull was an early activist for women's rights and labor reform. She was a leader in the American suffragist movement and was the first woman to run for president of the United States. In a speech given in 1871, she stated: "Have the courage of your convictions; don't mind what the world says; don't try to be popular...do your duty." Her life was a testament to questioning the status quo and living with passion and purpose.

It takes courage to act on these beliefs, because they might go up against what is expected of you. Anyone who's had influence on our behaviors and upbringing, from parents, teachers, and friends to the media, government, and religion, has helped to condition us for the life we're expected to live. And while these influencers might be well-intentioned people who love us, their cultivation is part of a group identity that is ensuring its own survival. Our society expects us to uphold the status quo and rely on outside "experts" rather than on ourselves and each other. It's threatening to suggest there might be alternate ways. We challenge this system when we question what we've been told and go out to explore the territory for ourselves. As philanthropists, it's our duty to redefine our personal good life so that others have the same opportunity.

Recognizing Ourselves as Other in Order to Help Others

As you begin to recognize that the terrain you inhabit is largely a construct that we, as a community, create and uphold, it becomes easier to see that the divisions between ourselves and others are also largely made up. Not taking as much, as a way to build up your good life, opens up a vast opportunity to recognize yourself in all the others that share this space. Adopting the mantras of "wanting less" and "having enough" in a simpler lifestyle, you can start to find ways to step away from the map you've been given in order to experience someone else's. And in experiencing someone else's, you soon realize that it's an overlay to the same underlying pattern. Engaging with others redraws our maps, which has the potential to change the landscape for both parties.

When I became a mother, I was completely lost without my usual tools of control. I had been thrust into a wildness I didn't recognize, and my trusty old map of how to do things no longer served me. Everything felt dangerous, yet I continued to tiptoe deeper into the experience. And as I did, I began to read my surroundings and start the ongoing build of being in relationship with my child. Together we were creating a new landscape, no map needed. Immersing myself with no sense of direction (and in those early days, no concept of day or night) is when I started to trust myself and use the navigational tools that were internal but untapped. A shared operating system that comes from slowing down and being present.

There was a night I remember so well, when I sat up with my son who was sick and vomiting. I rocked with him, listening to his soft moaning as he fell into a light sleep before he woke to vomit again. And in the darkness, listening to the rhythmic creaking of the chair back and forth, I was every mother everywhere. I could feel it in my cells as surely as I could feel the weight of my child and the hot breath against my neck. In that moment, my world shifted. There was no separation between me and every other mother across space and time. There was a book I used to read to my boys called *All Mommies*, simple pictures of different animals and their offspring. It was a counting book and each page repeated the pattern, a mommy cow loves her calf, a mommy rabbit loves her bunnies, until the end where a little boy is running toward his mother: all mommies love their babies. A gauze lifted on a part of nature that I'd been more than willing to ignore for my own pleasure and benefit. I felt kinship with the cows who labored to deliver, who looked down on what they had created, only to see their child taken from them. I felt connected to the mommy hedgehogs and deer, and I saw my map merge with theirs and our destinies became one and the same. I was standing at the epicenter of creation and love, which was forcing me to reckon with my own desires versus that of another being.

And then there was the picture of the little boy drowned off the coast of Greece trying to escape the war in Syria. I had been successfully avoiding this particular picture because I knew it would crush my heart into a million pieces. I had a similarly aged boy playing on the kitchen floor and I couldn't bear the thought of it. Yet when the picture flashed in front of me one afternoon, I didn't click away. I forced myself to look at it, and in doing so I let the world rush in. I sat and grieved, uncontrollable weeping, and the crisis in Syria was made personal. I could no longer be content in my own terrain with my own map. I asked myself how I could be of use to mothers half a world away. How could we be a welcoming family to others coming here from horrible situations? How could I bring this pain so deeply inside of me that it would redraw my map?

The initial responses to these questions were easy enough actions: we provided Christmas gifts to a refugee family in our town, we made a small financial donation to the White Helmets, and I signed the petition urging the UN Security Council to introduce a "no fly zone" if necessary. I also sent our baby carrier to Carry Our Future to be delivered to a family arriving in Greece. These actions were not written up on my giving plan, but they did align with my passions and vision for a better world. I was using my philanthropic plan to spontaneously engage with the territory that unfolded in front of me: this is where the magic happens. Being in relationship (with another person, an environment, a time) is the only way to participate in the dance of giving and receiving. And while there is space for both the controlled experience and being open to the moment, the skill is in toggling between knowing how to use the map to get to where you want to go and knowing when to put it down and experience a back road. My giving portfolio could flex with resources I had at hand (political action, donating an item, providing gifts) because I chose to be a witness to another, and in so doing recognized myself.

How do these actions make any difference in the overall crisis though? Do they merely make me feel good, enabling me to turn back to my life with a clear conscience that I "did something"? It's complicated, and I'm not sure there's a clear answer that will make sense to every individual. When the problems are immense, and quite frankly more political in nature, it's hard to find a way to make a difference. But engaging with the problem and getting involved on a local and personal level is something. While this may appear Pollyanna-ish, it's the only way the majority of individuals can shift the narrative. When the issues are beyond our control or comprehension, and we feel overwhelmed with our inability to help on global or systemic issues, sometimes it's all we can do to help one person or plant one tree. My belief is that it's our ability to connect to the systemic issues, while recognizing ourselves in others and helping from that place, which will ultimately shift the larger political sphere.

True philanthropy isn't about altruism or charity, which for all the good they might do, are still ego-based actions because you are doing good from a position of power and privilege. True philanthropy is recognizing that you are everywhere and everywhere is in you. The self melts away and there is no "you" to give. You are the drowned boy on the beach, the cow giving birth, the glaciers melting. From this place, your giving is about being one with the world. And this is how we change the conversation.

Wangari Maathai founded the Green Belt Movement in the 1970s, initially as encouragement for rural Kenyan women to work together to grow seedlings and plant trees, in response to their concern about the streams drying up, food supply becoming less secure, and the need to walk farther and farther to get firewood. Planting trees was the first step toward greater agency for these women, which evolved first into seminars on civic and environmental education, then greater democratic space and more accountability from national leaders. After Maathai received the Nobel Peace Prize in 2004, the Green Belt Movement burst onto the international stage and has been able to expand its community development work, including environmental conservation, democracy, community empowerment, and conflict resolution. I remember reading an article in grad school where she was quoted as saying: "As for me, I've made a choice." I think of this simple statement often, that making a choice to be a part of the solution might just start with planting one tree, but if you comprehend the larger picture and how this act might be the leverage to greater change, your choice to get involved could result in significant global impact.

Working for Justice in Order to be Generous

Ironing out the ways that your actions perpetuate inequalities is the only way to ensure that your generosity will create real change. Doing this work is an ongoing cycle of action and reflection, a constant personal evolution that usually takes iterations and a lifetime of learning. Sustainable change happens incrementally, through small actions that build. Sometimes changes look like they happened overnight, but more often than not they are the crest of a wave that had been building, slowly, under the surface. It is this movement of individuals *under the surface*, who are making personal choices and acting on those choices, who will generate long-term justice and equity.

Generosity on its own misses the mark, because the action of generosity untethered from justice is ignorance veiled in hands-off compassion. This kind of generosity ensures that these issues will remain entrenched; inequity exists in the corners, in the policies, and ingrained power dynamics of our communities. Explicitly addressing the disparities that divide us, albeit difficult work, helps to unearth all that connects us. Your solidarity with others means you are building bridges across issues, communities, and movements, and are aware of the unique concerns that manifest at the intersections. You truly join others when you become conscientious of the language you use and how you listen and offer support.

There are a plethora of resources to guide you on a personal journey to uncover hidden biases and locate unquestioned assumptions. You can begin by doing a personal audit of how you show up. This might be participating in rallies, speaking out on social media, signing petitions, or reading voices that represent different viewpoints. Your presence in the conversation matters, both in person and virtually. When we stay in our own safe places, surrounded by people who think and look like us, we remain siloed in our passions. Our generosity here feels good, but it's questionable whether we're moving the needle on anything. Take an issue you care about and hold up another lens, see what nuance this adds. One of the places I've had to deepen my generosity is in issues impacting women and girls. Using the lens of women of color I came to realize that I'd been staying safely in the shallow end of feminism. It didn't occur to me that there was such a thing as "white feminism" until I held up a mirror. And in using the lens of men and boys, I've been able to see that my feminism was rooted in a story of victim and perpetrator rather than a system of inequity that hurts us all.

Once you've begun to move more confidently into the territory, you can encourage others to join you by holding space for their change as well. We all have this power, to be the container for someone else to come into their full expression of generosity, which works for justice and shifts our focus from doing philanthropy to being a philanthropist. By doing the work, and inviting others in, you become a part of something, which is the only way to truly understand it. Without this experience, you are a bystander at best and at worst, a voyeur. There are things we don't want to know about the world, things we don't want to admit about ourselves. People are distressed and grieving, acting violently, behaving selfishly. The world is messy in its imperfections. But wading in and forcing ourselves to stay aware, looking at the picture of the drowned three-year-old boy on the beach or understanding women's issues from the perspective of women who don't look like you, emboldens us to do better. By not looking away from another person's experience, you honor them and acknowledge your shared humanity. Cultivating this humanity opens you to the possibility of another person's truth. This empathy is not merely seeing from another's perspective, it's the ability to value and respect another person even if you don't agree with them. It's recognizing that caring about another's well-being is just as important as your own happiness. And through this balance between your happiness and another's, you are able to expand your generosity.

Philanthropy is the action of giving yourself to the world. Being present in conversations and convenings of equity and justice allow you to viscerally feel the truth in the statement, "When one of us suffers, we all suffer." Our futures are intertwined with everything on this earth, and everything we love is at stake. Your generosity is nothing if it's not rooted in that awareness, if it's not built on a foundation of action as an expression of your commitment to justice. Becoming informed, intentional, and joyful with your philanthropy is the ongoing exercise of distilling your beliefs into an actionable plan that encompasses activism and social justice. Honestly engaging with the territory of your philanthropy, using all of your resources, deepens your desire to change the landscape. Everything personal is political. You are going from *how to give and receive* to *how to disrupt the system*.

CHAPTER TWELVE
A Systems Perspective

"The gift you carry for others is not an attempt to save the world but to fully belong to it. It's not possible to save the world by trying to save it. You need to find what is genuinely yours to offer the world before you can make it a better place. Discovering your unique gift to bring to your community is your greatest opportunity and challenge. The offering of that gift—your true self—is the most you can do to love and serve the world. And it is all the world needs."

—Bill Plotkin, *Soulcraft: Crossing Into the Mysteries of Nature and Psyche*

EVERYTHING AROUND us makes up a system of one sort or another. From our nervous system to our solar system, from trash collection agencies to day care centers, from local governments to the UN, simple and complex systems are operating all around us. Punctuating these tangible systems are the more esoteric ones—systems that are racial, ecological, economic, societal. A system is any group of interacting, interrelated, or interdependent parts that form a complex and unified whole that has a specific purpose. Your body is a system, your family is a system, and your neighborhood is a system—all fitting together like a nesting doll producing emergent patterns of collective behavior. A system is not merely a collection of things (your body goes together in a very precise and specific way); it is more than just the sum of its parts. For each system there are positive and negative feedback loops that provide information and control, and many of these interact with each other (in fact the only way to have a healthy system is for positive and negative loops to work together, keeping each one in check from running a system amok).

It helps in a discussion of systems to also understand how they fit within a broader context. I was taught to imagine an iceberg, where the events we can see and respond to are merely the tip above the water. This is our shared reality. Just under the water are the patterns of events we might gain access to if we pay attention to cycles and trends; these patterns create a historical picture of what and why our shared reality exists as it does. Forming the bottom of the iceberg, so far under the water it's invisible to those on the surface, are systemic structures. These systemic structures are the bedrock of our societal networks and norms, and remain beyond comprehension for most of us, a cultural and tribal identity that we are hard-pressed to "see." In order to create a new shared reality and disrupt the tangible events on the surface, it's necessary to intervene at the lowest level of systemic structures. For example, The Center for Social Innovation documented that people of color are more likely to experience homelessness than whites, even when controlled for poverty, and this inequity is the direct result of systemic racism. Therefore, without confronting the racial roots of homelessness, from housing and employment discrimination to disproportionality in the criminal justice and child welfare systems, efforts to eradicate homelessness (the event above the water) will ultimately fail. It's not always as simple as giving someone a home, as I stated earlier, when there are other systems working against that individual. Providing a home is valuable, only if you are making changes to the unseen part of the iceberg as well. Dismantling the barriers at this systemic level is the only way to create the necessary paradigm shift that influences real change.

Taking a systems approach provides you with a wider snapshot of the world. It gives a multidimensional understanding of context and the actions of people and events. It insists that you know your place in the system and keeps you open to the possibility that your perspective is skewed based on your vantage point (whether privileged or not). Understanding systems and how they behave provides you with the tools to work with them, rather than being controlled by them, in order to create equity and quality of life. Coming to see the systemic structures we live within puts you in a constant state of recalibration of your knowledge and understanding, and provides compassion for the actions of people and the events of our world. Your evolution as a philanthropist is continually opening you to new ways of being, acknowledging the complexity and your complicity. By rooting yourself in generosity and deep empathy, for yourself and others, you can begin to ask, as Darren Walker, president of the Ford Foundation, did: "What can we do to leverage our privilege to disrupt the drivers of inequality?"

While not all of us are going to be social entrepreneurs innovating life-changing solutions, we can look for the ways to disrupt the drivers of inequality in our own lives. We can all be informed about the issues and choose to do something that leverages our privilege to make life better. Take again the example of babies floating down the river. You might educate yourself about the people running for office and vote for the person who will fix the bridge. Maybe you decide to run for office yourself. You might be able to provide other resources like a car for people to go up river and divert traffic, or maybe the materials to make signage. Maybe you spend your days pulling babies from the river. Each of these actions alone won't solve the whole problem, but they address a part. And each part is in itself a whole, just as saving one baby means the world to one mother or father.

Of course, the river and the babies are just a metaphor for anything going wrong in our world. Does your child's school have resources galore while five miles away another school doesn't have a playground set? Is there a piece of green space in your neighborhood that a community group is trying to save from developers? Is there a protest taking place outside your office to support immigrants and refugees? As you get involved on the ground, you further educate yourself about the system and the injustices being perpetrated in each of these scenarios. It might seem impossible to solve a global crisis, but you can reach out to one person and make a difference. You can find one situation that doesn't seem right and find a way to get involved. Doing something for one is the way to the many. Becoming an engaged philanthropist means recognizing that change can happen up and down the spectrum: behavior changes of an individual and collective change between individuals and groups of individuals. There is a place for both approaches, and there are different people for the roles, and at different times. What is ultimately important to the success of either approach is working toward a shift in the underlying systemic structure. In this way, by paying attention to the whole while taking care of a part, we are living our philanthropy.

My point is this. Know yourself and your resources and find ways to apply them to the whole or the part or the pattern, toggling along the continuum dependent on the situation, recognizing that other people are playing different roles. Underpinning all of this is the need for more individuals to wake up to their power in philanthropy, to continue to inform themselves about the larger issues and find ways to connect with each other and across needs. Since beginning this work,

I have come full circle and back again: there are days I can only imagine the impact of a system-wide approach and at other times I realize the only way to accomplish anything is to change the individual. Each point of contact is an entry point to an entire universe.

CHAPTER THIRTEEN
The Hive: Using Feminist Philanthropy to Change the World

PHILANTHROPY IS evolving into a social movement of changemakers and activists, rather than transactions and networks of do-gooders. Like an artist, your contribution is dependent first on the skills you've honed and the resources and information you've gathered, but it is worth nothing if it stays in your head and is not available for the world to participate in. In order to elevate your generosity to an art form, to create a beautiful thing that will change hearts and minds, you must be ready to put yourself in the picture.

This is the philanthropy of the twenty-first century, a feminist philanthropy that is relationship based and holistic, seeking long-term, systemic change over short-term outcomes and individual objectives. It transforms the giver, the receiver, and the situation of need. It is a lifestyle. Marion Weber, the founder of The Flow Fund Circle, speaks of "catalyst philanthropists" who will "empower the earth's visionaries and initiators...(who will be) magnetized together into different groups." The goal is to make being a philanthropist "common and seen as just one form of extending generosity" and to create "a great healing instead of hoarding of money". Weber's vision for the future of philanthropy is similar to my own: that a cascade of individuals will rise up and make generosity integral to their daily routines in a way that is intentional and aligned with their passions, while responding to community needs and tackling systemic problems.

This is where philanthropy can capitalize on the evolution of the social media model, operating as a hive rather than a network. Where a network provides tools for information sharing and connecting solely for the sake of connections, the hive elevates the ability of collective action toward outcomes, emerging in real time. From cloud computing to blockchain technology, we are witnessing a radical change in how we share and store information and exchange value. The decentralized database allows individuals to create transactions peer-to-peer, with the potential to strengthen relationships and highlight the problems worth solving, as well as the solutions. Centralized institutions, like banks and retailers, are in the midst of a sea change, not only in *how* they do business, but ultimately what their business is about. Think of the evolution of how we listen to music, how we send money, how we call a cab or purchase shoes. Technology is going to create decentralized and spontaneous opportunities, with implications for many industries and institutions, including philanthropy. This is the hive, and hive philanthropy is bigger than the sum of its parts.

In a hive, insects perform a specific role for the good of the group. They often appear to be drawing from a larger intelligence that is tapped into, or reading the subtle cues that go unnoticed by others. Watching a flight of birds swooping over a field in choreographed dance, it appears that they are magnetized together. Humans, when tapped into our shared existence, have this ability to read each other, to recognize our commonalities and act for the good of the whole community. While this might mean putting aside our individual desires, it doesn't mean we need to subjugate our individual rights and idiosyncrasies. A hive mindset provides individuals with the opportunity to contribute and work toward a shared goal; it gives each of us a role and asks that we participate. And with the help of our evolving technology, individuals can swarm around a problem and create immediate change that to an onlooker would appear as a choreographed dance of giving.

Before hive philanthropy can truly take flight, however, we need to define our shared goal. In our increasingly polarized world, this is no easy feat. But in each sector, leaders are coming together and setting bold visions for changing the world. If you take food security as an example, you can break it all down into parts: food banks, food deserts, food stamps, etc. But take a step back. Consider what we're really discussing. Food is a basic human right, just like water and shelter and safety. Those without food aren't less than those of us who can shop at a multitude of grocery stores. I have at least seven well-stocked grocery stores within a five-mile radius of my house—*seven*. The issue here is not that there isn't enough. The problem is not a lack of food in our country. In fact, I'd wager there is an overabundance of wasted food. The simplicity of the issue looms large in my mind and I begin to ask questions: Where does all this food go? Where does it come from? Why is it consolidated here, when there are neighborhoods without any? Who is in charge of these decisions? Why can't good food be available to everyone? What levers are in place that could change this?

The answers to these questions range from simple to complex, depending on how deep you want to go and in what direction. There are issues of poverty, and issues of racism, and issues of capitalism and economics and power. We forget (as we witness the events from the top of the iceberg) that our world is not static, and the events we see today have roots in a systemic structure. In the case of the "food desert" the systems are racial and economic. Fixing a systemic issue with an "event"-based solution (bringing in a grocery store or fresh produce truck), while necessary to aid immediate need, doesn't address the underlying problem, which is that the food system is a broken system. The politics of poverty, racism, and food scarcity play out across a community spectrum—what will it take to change this issue? Could grocery stores integrate with food banks so that we all shop at the same place? Could food banks be keepers of food salvaging and community gardens to feed those in immediate, but temporary, need? Could educational systems incorporate gardening and cooking classes into their curriculums?

While these might be Band-Aids, addressing the events and patterns of the iceberg, they begin to connect the nodes across a wide spectrum of need, evolving from a network of services to a hive of action. And by connecting nodes, the bigger issues emerge: providing a livable wage, affordable childcare and housing. Just like many other social and planetary challenges, it's a matter of will and logistics. We don't have a shortage of resources, we just need to unleash our imaginations and ask *what's possible*. To fix a broken system, a community needs to first agree that something is broken. In this scenario, the shared goal could be to ensure everyone has access to healthy, affordable food. This might mean policy changes, corporate changes, individual changes. If racism and power are underlying components to food insecurity, the recognition of the "ethnic food" signage at your grocery store is an entry point. From whose perspective was this sign created? All of these recognitions matter. The goal to "save more babies from drowning" has a much different approach than the goal to "pull more babies from the water." It opens the possibility that there are underlying issues at play. Pulling babies from the river solves a problem, sure. Yet it avoids the most important questions and misses an opportunity to create real change.

The second component of an emerging hive philanthropy is shifting the status quo by grappling with our role in inequity and our islands of privilege. To be a part of any worthy solution, you must first name and own the part you have in the problem. My husband and I were discussing this privilege the other night as we pored over our bills, trying to make a few ends meet and addressing where we're overspending. We talk to each other about our "vow of poverty" when I decided to stay home full-time to raise the boys in their early years, and our experience living on one salary. But the truth is, many people live on much less, often on two salaries. We may drive a used car, wear our clothes until they fall apart, shop discounts and rely on hand-me-downs and consignment, but when we look around at what we have and what we're able to do, we absolutely do not live in poverty. It's disingenuous to joke about it.

I've begun to consider, however, that this vow of poverty is actually an attempt at living lightly. That the true meaning of "vow of poverty" is living a simple lifestyle outside the system of production and consumption. It is an inquiry into living without the trappings of our privilege, and making choices that reflect and support a different belief system. One that places us as one agent in a system, not more or less. Because, of course, we are afforded the opportunity of the upper middle class not just by choices we've made but by the social, political, and racial construct into which we were born. Our choices are not feasible for the majority of Americans, let alone the world. Even the choice to live "without the trappings of our privilege" is a privilege. Indeed, our "choices" might not really be choices at all. We have more than enough, which is why this work is very personal for me. I see many of my friends and neighbors living in this land of "enough" and "more than enough" and still struggling to make a good life. We increasingly find ourselves asking, *Is this it? What am I really here to do?*

Hive philanthropists answer these questions by knowing exactly what they have and what they have to give. They are independent cells activated by a well-defined problem, ready to act with a clear role to play. Essential to their success is commitment to community connections and trust. Increased technological efficiencies support the transaction component of this work, but it is the inclusion and relationship that makes this model transformational. A hive is only successful when each member contributes to the health of the whole, and this is done when we believe that each of us is a whole unto ourselves, and just as necessary to the functioning of the hive as anyone else. It is a beautiful arrangement that benefits not just the hive but the entire ecosystem in which it resides.

Embedded within this hive model are the feminist principles of solidarity, agency, and reciprocity. We stand together because we are all one, we honor each other as experts in our own lives, and we give and receive as a fluid act of appreciation for all that is. This philanthropy engages a systems perspective, one that shifts our narrative from one of extraction to one of cocreation, and centers our giving and receiving on wholeness and equity. Feminist philanthropy has arisen from a movement of people who demand to be a voice at the table and to recognize nature as a guide. When you approach your giving from this perspective, you're able to align your privilege with purpose.

Feminist philanthropy is relational by nature. It pulls people in and creates a shared agenda, linking everyone together rather than ranking them (the division between those giving and those receiving fades to elevate a mutually beneficial goal). And the hive is a metaphor for this activity: across class, race, and gender lines, we are better off when we work together. By creating mutual respect and acknowledging the intersection of issues while holding a shared vision, we cultivate a culture of inclusivity and safety. The power of feminist philanthropy lies in this: nurturing a culture of relationship and connection allows for creative and innovative expression to flourish, and this expression will change the world.

To that end, a feminist philanthropist has done the personal work to bring her whole self to the community, and in doing so is able to heal the problems of her environment. Her eyes are open to the constructs within which we live and operate, the ones that provide privilege and benefit to some and not to others. She asks herself how she can place her philanthropy at the front end of the system rather than trying to create solutions and provide resources at the back end. When we're not actively questioning our role in the problem, we're not actually working to be a part of the solution. Tackling the circumstances of economic and social injustice, which make philanthropy necessary, starts with acknowledging our participation in the systems. It begins when we recognize our privilege, and takes off when we apply ourselves to dismantling the construct we benefit from at the expense of others. Getting clear with ourselves about our intentions, quieting the ego, and listening and learning are the ways of the hive, and the work of feminist philanthropy.

It's important to note that feminist philanthropy is not merely female-powered giving circles or exclusively funding "female" issues (birth control, domestic violence, and sex trafficking, by the way, are not solely female issues). Many of these giving vehicles and the people interacting with them are still operating under the old philanthropic model of transactional, reactionary giving. Just being a woman who gives does not automatically make you a feminist philanthropist; indeed, many men and gender nonconforming individuals are using the tools of feminism to create a more intersectional and relational experience of giving. I purposefully use the pronouns she/her throughout this book because so many of our documents automatically use he/him. This use of pronouns is one step in my journey, still being traveled.

We live in a pivotal moment in time, one that is both connecting us beyond our wildest imaginations and dividing us with scarcity and fear. The challenges of connection and community are at the heart of philanthropy, our human response to loving each other. Our intentional commitment, as feminist philanthropists who are part of a healthy hive, is to craft structures, institutions, and human realities that cultivate justice, simplicity and peace. Your generous heart yearns to give more; it wants to give as much as possible. This heart sustains our vision for the long term and as we strengthen it, "we are called to be architects of the future, not its victims."

CHAPTER FOURTEEN
In Conclusion

"Those on the edge hold the key to healing and uniting the whole system."

—Tim Shriver

IN 2004, my graduate studies were in (at that time) Whole Systems Design, an oft misunderstood study of systems. I was taking classes titled Nature as Metaphor and Notating Imagination, learning about Participatory Design, Appreciative Inquiry and Action Research, reading Fritjof Capra's *The Web of Life* and Gregory Bateson's *Steps to an Ecology of Mind*. But people assumed Whole Systems Design had something to do with computer science. I was immersed in a study of systems theory and how it applied to everything around me. The overlay of this education was my interest in issues pertaining to women and girls and my work at the time founding a nonprofit. I came away with undeniable proof that we cannot do something without it creating unintended consequences somewhere else. All good can look evil, depending on what side of the table you sit. Further, the labels themselves were arbitrary when it came to nature. It's all a system working toward an outcome that we may or may not fully understand, or appreciate. My contribution toward establishing peace for individuals and communities comes from helping to restore the wisdom of philanthropy.

The essence of philanthropy is about reconnecting with each other, which includes the political and environmental impact of humans. The great mission of our time is to reidentify with a culture of giving rather than a culture of taking. It's a personal shift in consciousness, recognizing that the way we've been doing things isn't natural, and it isn't working. Our economy is built on social, racial, and environmental injustice, and as it's currently promoted, philanthropy is born out of this economic framework. Waking up to this fact allows us to do something different, and people are beginning to act on this knowledge across multiple platforms. We are searching for ways to interact with our world without exploiting and depleting it. As Jennifer and Peter Buffett, copresidents of the NoVo Foundation, stated, "When so much of our social fabric appears to be frayed, the solution is not to sew faster but to find new material."

Our best leaders, artists, and innovators are learning how to mimic nature in order to create more sustainable, equitable systems for a thriving planet. Superorganisms, like mushrooms, beehives, and coral reefs, are individual organisms being studied because of their ability to act as a singular organism. These are organisms that couldn't survive on their own but operate effectively together. And the fact that superorganisms create abundance where other organisms find scarcity presents us with a metaphor for the future of hivemind philanthropy. Tamsin Woolley-Barker eloquently explains the strength and innovation of superorganisms in an article for the Biomimicry Institute:

> For one thing, [superorganisms] build their compounding wealth on infinite things—sunlight and sugars, for example, and the complexity, diversity, and interconnectedness of networks. They grow from the edges out,

adding modular, self-managed units that seek and respond to opportunity and threat on the front lines. Team performance emerges in real-time, like a constantly updated film-reel of snapshots built from thousands of pixels. Superorganisms break large, complex problems into tiny bites of action, building until tipping points are reached and change is triggered. There are no forecasts, budgets, meetings, or plans. There is no boss. Strategy happens organically, all the time, everywhere, and decisions are frequent, small, and imperfect. This is how superorganisms adapt to change—at the edges, all the time, in little bits of work done by everyone.

So it can be for philanthropists with a clear giving philosophy: find your infinite resource, the thing that comes easily to you, and put it into practice in order to be a self-managed unit responding in real time, as opportunities present themselves. As we become clear about our place in this network, we jointly make frequent, small, and imperfect decisions as we work toward the tipping point. As we acknowledge that we inhabit a finite Earth, the power of the superorganism philanthropist is that she is able to convert whatever resources she has into something useful for someone else. This is how the wealth of what you already have compounds. "In nature's economy," writes Vandiva Shiva, "the currency is not money, it is life."

Philanthropy is evolving to address the disparities from which it is born and makes necessary. Impact investing and corporate social responsibility are just one iteration of the conversation. With movements like shop/eat local and Together Rising's Love Flash Mobs, people are questioning the way in which we use money. If money is merely the tool that makes our life force tangible, we have complete control of what this system should look like, because *we are the system*. Similar to Wendell Berry asserting that "[t]here is no distinction between ourselves and the so-called environment," money is an extension of us, part of a system that we have created. Berry goes on to state, "What we live in and from and with doesn't surround us—it's part of us. We're of it and it's of us, and the relationship is unspeakably intimate." Being aware of yourself as a singular organism, one part of a whole superorganism, gives you the entry point to change. You are the leverage the world needs as it moves toward the tipping point.

So many of us feel that we're not doing enough for a world in desperate need of help. We are overstretched and fatigued by the amount of responsibilities, real and perceived, we feel we should be attending to. We don't just learn of the individual down the street who lost their house to a fire, we learn of the mountain towns of India rocked by earthquakes and the thousands of girls sold into sex slavery. How do we find ways to help? How do we help others without depleting ourselves, leaving us feeling helpless with donor fatigue? How do we conduct ourselves, every day, as informed, intentional, and joyful philanthropists?

The answer is simply, be a philanthropist. Be generous, be thoughtful, be compassionate. With yourself first, then the people around you, then further out into the world. There is power in declaring yourself a philanthropist and embracing the title, taking the meaning of the word back to its roots: love people and promote the welfare of humanity. We are all needed in this story of humanity because we all give voice to unique aspects of need. All over the world, our communities are changing and our philanthropy needs to reflect this truth. Naming yourself a philanthropist is a political statement because it shifts the perception of what matters, and it places the individual in a position of power who can create solutions to address complex problems. Philanthropy was never meant to be an elite activity. It is an opportunity for all of us to connect to the deepest part of our legacies.

With the following five directives, you join a movement of change as a feminist philanthropist:

- **Affirm to yourself that you are a generous heart seeking to promote the welfare of others.** Take time to understand an issue from the perspective of those affected. Acknowledge that we are all experts in our own lives and not in someone else's. Then find ways to nurture your generous heart because you can't give what you don't have.
- **Put a stake in the sand and make a personal commitment to get involved with a streamlined list of issues.** Get creative with your available resources—look over your time, skills, connections, attention, as well as money.
- **Align your actions with your passions.** Let those passions/issues sit center stage in all the decisions and choices you make throughout your day. Do things that are meaningful.
- **Be happy with what you have.** Simplify your life by removing stuff and obligation. Be a creative giver, not a consumer.
- **Take pleasure in giving with no obligation or expectation.** Express gratitude for receiving and allow someone else the gift of providing. We are all grateful receivers and we all possess wealth.

You are a philanthropist. You are here to make a difference with your life and create a legacy of giving. Opportunities to give will emerge when you are in action, out in the world. Be informed and intentional with your giving, and joyful in your approach. As Desmond Tutu so simply told us, "Do your little bit of good where you are; it's those little bits of good put together that overwhelm the world."

Let's overwhelm.

Continue the conversation

This book is a start to the conversation around feminist philanthropy. I invite you to join my email newsletter at **kristencorningbedford.com** to keep this conversation going and stay in touch about new books, retreats, and more.

Gratitude

Writing this book has been a great labor of love and provided me such sustenance as I've transitioned from working full time to creating a new way of being after becoming a mother. There are so many people to thank for supporting me on this journey.

First, I need to thank Mariah Lincoln, who said to me on our drive back from Whidbey Island after my second philanthroBE retreat, "You need to write this into a book". Thank you for your words and subsequent encouragement – it set me on a path of creation that has been engaging, inspiring and fulfilling.

I appreciate all of my early readers who gave great feedback; two readers in particular were instrumental to the development and success of getting this thing completed. Erik Hanberg, whose enthusiasm for my philanthropy writing goes all the way back to my Exit133 blog post days in Tacoma, and whose more recent involvement as a co-publisher was above and beyond. Your thoughtful input and ongoing encouragement has meant so much to me, and it has been such fun sharing my first experience of publishing with you. And to Wendy Herlich who provided editing input at a pivotal point, shining a light on what was missing and what could be fixed. Your continued friendship is one of the most important gifts of my life.

To all the women who have come on my retreats, I appreciate the generosity of spirit in going on a journey with me and each other (and yourself!), and for sharing your dreams for a better world and helping me craft real stories about the struggles we encounter as everyday changemakers. Thank you to the Whidbey Institute and Heather Johnson for providing a gracious space to explore and connect.

Antioch University Seattle gave me the validation of my dreams. It was during my time there that I realized my worldview was shared and supported by many others. I received incredible instruction and resources to become a change agent and thought partner, paving a path the world was ready to take. A special thank you to one of my professors, Guy Burneko, who pushed me to articulate my own voice and vision, and told me he looked forward to seeing me in print someday. And to Sherman Alexie and Andrea Allen, who asked the tough questions while I was completing my master's degree and thesis. Andrea, you will always be my #bullshitador.

I am indebted to the many writers, leaders and entrepreneurs I quote and list in the resources and throughout this book. Your thinking has motivated and inspired my own writing and creating. Thank you for putting yourself into the world so that others have something to strive toward.

To my parents, Nic and Pat, and my sister, Lauren, who were my earliest and most consistent teachers on selflessness and generosity. To my inlaws, Norm and Norma, for expressing curiosity and excitement about my work, always.

I couldn't have written any of this without the love and support of my husband and kids. Slade, you believe in me more than anyone else and are a beacon that calls me home every day. Liam and Theo, you teach me what joyful generosity looks like and make it all the more important for me to be mindful of the future, for all of us. I love you all the way to Neptune in a rocketship that goes as slow as a snail.

Resources & Books

This is a sampling of the websites, organizations, and books that have been inspirational and informative in my philanthropic journey. They provide a solid platform for informed, intentional, and joyful giving. Use them as tools to continue exploring, and as a launching pad to generate your own big ideas.

(Please note, as technology continues to change the philanthropic landscape, please do your own research and use your best judgment when using any of the online or app tools. Their inclusion here is not an endorsement of their services, just that the ingenuity and evolution inspired my thinking.)

Action Checklist is a weekly newsletter that provides simple, well-researched actions to support democracy, voting access, and equality; acts of gratitude to praise elected officials doing good; good news about our democracy; and a short reading list of quality articles. jenniferhofmann.com/home/weekly-action-checklist-democrats-independents-republicans-conscience/

Allow Good empowers youth through the tools of philanthropy to take meaningful action in their world. www.allowgood.org

Apartment Therapy has an article written by professional organizer Amelia Meena which is a compilation of places to donate home goods and clothes as you simplify your life and want to contribute to others. www.apartmenttherapy.com/big-list-of-the-best-donation-centers-for-all-your-stuff-199469

The Art of Simple is a community-focused blog and podcast about working for the common good, pursuing margin, and savoring the little things in life. www.theartofsimple.net

Ashoka builds and cultivates a community of change leaders who understand that the world now requires everyone to be a changemaker. www.ashoka.org

Awesome Foundation is a global community of giving circles, "advancing the interest of awesome in the universe, $1000 at a time". Each fully autonomous chapter supports awesome projects through micro-grants, usually given out monthly. These micro-grants, $1000 or the local equivalent, come out of pockets of the chapter's "trustees" and are given on a no-strings-attached basis to people and groups working on awesome projects. www.awesomefoundation.org

BBB Wise Giving Alliance helps donors make informed giving decisions and promotes high standards of conduct among organizations that solicit contributions from the public. It produces reports about national charities, evaluating them against comprehensive Standards for Charity Accountability, and publishes a magazine, the *Wise Giving Guide*, three times a year. BBB WGA does not rank charities but seeks to assist donors in making informed judgments about those that solicit their support. Evaluations are done without charge to the charity and are posted for free public access give.org.

Bill Moyers.com includes a video archive of Bill Moyers's forty-plus year journalism career, offering nearly 1,000 archived programs, video clips, and online-original segments. It also features essays and videos from other journalists, scholars, activists, and creative men and women in the arts and sciences.

A Billion + Change is transforming business culture so that all companies in America will respond to the needs of their community and unleash the talent and expertise of their people in pro bono and skills-based service. www.abillionpluschange.org

Bioneers is an innovative nonprofit educational organization that highlights breakthrough solutions for restoring people and planet. Founded in 1990 in Santa Fe, New Mexico, by social entrepreneurs Kenny Ausubel and Nina Simons, Bioneers has acted as a fertile hub of social and scientific innovators with practical and visionary solutions for the world's most pressing environmental and social challenges. A celebration of the genius of nature and human ingenuity, Bioneers connects people with breakthrough solutions and each other. www.bioneers.org

Bolder Giving inspires and supports people to give at their full lifetime potential. www.morethanmoney.org and www.boldergiving.org

Brain Pickings is a record of Maria Popova's own becoming as a person—intellectually, creatively, spiritually—and an inquiry into how to live and what it means to lead a good life. Founded in 2006 as a weekly email that went out to seven friends and eventually brought online, the site was included in the Library of Congress permanent web archive in 2012. www.brainpickings.org

Buckminster Fuller Institute (BFI) is building on the profoundly relevant legacy of twentieth-century inventor, architect and global systems visionary, R. Buckminster Fuller. The Buckminster Fuller Institute (BFI) is dedicated to catalyzing transformative solutions to complex global problems through design thinking education. www.bfi.org

Buy Nothing Project is about setting the scarcity model of our cash economy aside in favor of creatively and collaboratively sharing the abundance around us. With Buy Nothing, local groups form gift economies that are complementary and parallel to local cash economies; whether people join because they'd like to quickly get rid of things that are cluttering their lives, or simply to save money by getting things for free, they quickly discover that the groups are not just another free recycling platform. www.buynothingproject.org

Catchafire provides individuals with talents and skills with meaningful pro bono experiences in order to build capacity for social good organizations. www.catchafire.org

New Dream is inspiring, engaging, and challenging Americans to reexamine their cultural values on consumption and consumerism and initiating a new national conversation around what "the good life" and the "American dream" mean. www.newdream.org

Charity Miles is an app that donates funds to nonprofits for every mile you move. Their members are active-ists, living healthy while helping others. www.charitymiles.org

CHIMP believes that giving changes the world, and that the more we give, the more we get back. Based in Vancouver, Canada, CHIMP connects people who want to make the world better with charities that are taking action on causes they care about. www.chimp.net

Community Sourced Capital (CSC) envisions a future that includes a more connected, equitable, and loving financial world. They connect, amplify, and educate people and communities around healthy finance. www.communitysourcedcapital.com

Community Supported Agriculture (CSA) allows you to buy local, seasonal food directly from a farmer. A farmer offers a certain number of shares (aka a 'membership' or 'subscription') to the public. Typically the share consists of a box of vegetables, but other farm products may be included. Locate one near you: www.localharvest.org/csa

Council on Foundations is an active philanthropic network of grantmaking foundations and corporations, founded in 1949. It provides the opportunity, leadership, and tools needed by philanthropic organizations to expand, enhance, and sustain their ability to advance the common good. www.cof.org

D5 is a five-year coalition to advance philanthropy's diversity, equity and inclusion. Their website provides resources and actions to help understand and support the rich variety of perspectives in order to achieve greater impact. www.d5coalition.org

DEED is an app that makes volunteering easy, fun and social. Upon signing up, you can explore local, high-impact volunteering opportunities near you and give back to your community in a variety of ways. apps.apple.com/us/app/deed-app/id1116827022

Do Something harnesses the energy of teens by creating a national call to action almost every week that doesn't require money, an adult, or a car. www.dosomething.org

Eat Well Guide is a curated directory of over 25,000 hand-picked restaurants, farms, markets and other sources of local, sustainable food throughout the US. The Guide's thousands of listings include restaurants, farms, farmers' markets, stores, and more. Search by location and/or category, or check out their city guides to find tailored listings for restaurants and other sustainable vendors in cities across the US. www.eatwellguide.org

Flow Funding, where donors entrust their money to social innovators and visionaries to give away. Flow Funding is a way to empower numerous new philanthropists to place strategic grants that are heartfelt and effective. www.flowfunding.org

Generation Waking Up is igniting a generation of young people to bring forth a thriving, just, sustainable world. www.generationwakingup.org

Giving Circles Network assists Giving Circles and other individual donors in making their contributions more meaningful. www.givingcircles.org

Giving Compass organizes the world's information about nonprofits and social change to make it easier to give well. They provide articles and research for philanthropists to do their own comparative research and learning, while joining with others who share their interests. www.givingcompass.org

Giving What We Can is an international society dedicated to eliminating poverty in the developing world. Their members understand that their comparative wealth can prevent a significant amount of suffering, so they each take a pledge to give at least 10% of their income to organizations in the developing world. www.givingwhatwecan.org

Global Fund for Women is a global champion for the human rights of women and girls. They use their powerful network to find, fund, and amplify the work of women who are building social movements and challenging the status quo. www.globalfundforwomen.org

Global Greengrants Fund is a network of changemakers that seeds environmental action through small grants. They act as a bridge between people seeking social justice and environmental sustainability by channeling donations to local projects and grassroots campaigns, primarily in the developing world and emerging economies. www.greengrants.org

GuideStar is the world's largest source of information on nonprofit organizations. Their nonprofit profiles provide information on funding, staffing and mission so that you can make informed decisions about what to support. www.guidestar.org

Kind Spring provides a wealth of ideas on how to change the world through small actions of kindness. www.kindspring.org/ideas

Inspired Legacies helps donors, advisors, and nonprofits collaborate for inspired outcomes for self, family, and society. www.inspiredphilanthropy.com

Intercommunity Peace & Justice Center was founded in 1991 as a collaborative venture to address issues of peace and justice. The Intercommunity Peace & Justice Center is sponsored by twenty-two religious communities and collaborates with Catholic, ecumenical, interfaith, and other organizations in carrying out its mission. www.ipjc.org

KarmaPay is a distributed fundraising platform that allows you to pay for what you want, then uses the proceeds for charity. This is an app that uses blockchain technology to activate everyday philanthropists by using global commerce to drive large-scale social change. www.karmapayapp.com

Kiva is an international nonprofit that connects people through lending to alleviate poverty. By lending as little as $25 on Kiva, anyone can help a borrower start or grow a business, go to school, access clean energy, or realize their potential. One hundred percent of every dollar you lend on Kiva goes to funding loans. www.kiva.org

Labyrinths reduce stress, quiets the mind and opens the heart. It is a walking meditation that follows the same path in as it follows out. Locate a labyrinth near you: http://labyrinthlocator.com/

Local Investing Opportunities Network (LION) creates opportunities for local businesses, nonprofits, and citizens to network. Their mission is to build prosperous local businesses, keep investing money in their community, and help build a more resilient and sustainable economy in East Jefferson County. www.l2020.org/economic-localization/lion

Moonjar and Money Savvy Pig are banks that teach kids how to view money as something to save, spend and share. www.amightygirl.com/money-savvy-pig and www.moonjar.com

National Philanthropic Trust provides a history of modern philanthropy www.historyofgiving.org/

Network for Good provides a donation calculator that tells you how your giving matches with other Amercian households. Eighty-nine percent of American households give to charity, with gifts averaging 3.2% of income, or $1,620 annually. How does your giving match up? www.networkforgood.org/donate/calculator/

Pledge Bank was a mySociety project, running from

2005–2015. It let people set up pledges in the form: "I pledge to _____ if x people will pledge to _____."
www.pledgebank.com/

Seeds For Change Network is a nonprofit training and support co-op helping people organize for action and positive social change. The network started in 2000 with informal cooperation between people who were doing workshops in their spare time. www.seedsforchange.org.uk

The Soul of Money Institute provides transformational and educational programs that inspire and empower individuals, organizations, and institutions to: align the acquisition and allocation of their financial resources with their most deeply held values; move from an economy of fear, consumption, and scarcity, to an economy of sufficiency, sustainability, and generosity; generate an expanding flow of resources toward the affirmation of life and the common good. www.soulofmoney.org

Stanford Social Innovation Review is a print magazine and online resource, informing and inspiring leaders of social change. They consistently provide thought provoking and inspirational ideas from the front lines of global philanthropic transformation. www.ssir.org

StartSomeGood is a crowdfunding platform where individuals can create change and grow community through innovative partnerships and social entrepreneur education. www.startsomegood.com

Story Of Stuff, Changemaker Quiz: Are you a networker, a resister, a builder? Take the changemaker personality quiz to see how you show up in the world and what role you play in creating change.

www.action.storyofstuff.org/survey/changemaker-quiz/

TimeBanks: In 1980, Edgar Cahn dreamed up a new kind of money. This new money would have no price: every hour would count the same. 1 hour = 1 hour. Passionate about social justice, Edgar saw timebanking as a way to restore community, to recognize and reward civic engagement. In the decades that followed, he became its strong, persistent champion, promoting timebanking as a tool for creating a more just, more caring world. In 1995 he founded the Time Dollar Institute—now known as TimeBanks USA—to promote timebanking in the US and around the world. www.timebanks.org

VolunteerMatch strengthens communities by matching inspiring people with inspiring causes. They offer a variety of online services to support nonprofits, volunteers and business leaders committed to civic engagement. www.volunteermatch.org

Books

Biomimicry, Janine M. Benyus

Birth of the Chaordic Age, Dee Hock

Braiding Sweetgrass, Robin Wall Kimmerer

Community: The Structure of Belonging, Peter Block

Give Smart: Philanthropy That Gets Results, Thomas J. Tierney and Joel L. Fleishman

Half the Sky, Nicholas D. Kristof and Sheryl WuDunn

If Women Rose Rooted, Sharon Blackie

Inspired Philanthropy, Tracy Gary

Paradigm Found: Leading and Managing for Positive Change, Anne Firth Murray

Read and Riot: A Pussy Riot Guide to Activism, Nadya Tolokonnikova

Sacred Economics, Charles Eisenstein

Small is Beautiful: Economics as if People Mattered, E. F. Shumacher

So You Want to Talk About Race, Ijeoma Oluo

Soul of Money, Lynne Twist

The Gifts of Imperfection, Brené Brown

The Seeker's Guide, Elizabeth Lesser

The Web of Life, Fritjof Capra

Think, Lisa Bloom

Your Money or Your Life, Vicki Robin and Joe Dominguez

Works Cited

Atwood, M. (2007). *Moral Disorder*. Anchor Books.

Berry, W. (2007) *Conversations with Wendell Berry*. University Press of Mississippi

Blackie, S. (2016). *If Women Rose Rooted*. Denmark: September Publishing.

Blake, W. (1757-1827) *The Marriage of Heaven and Hell*. Retrieved from https://poets.org/poem/proverbs-hell

Buffet, J. & P. (2015) https://www.philanthropy.com/article/Opinion-Philanthropy-Must/228019

Cornish, A., & Shapiro, A. (2016, December 1). *NPR*. Retrieved from NPR.org: http://www.npr.org/2016/12/01/504033613/giving-tuesday-generates-record-number-of-charitable-donations

Council on Foundations. (n.d.). Retrieved from http://www.cof.org/community-foundation-locator

Elgin, D. (2010) *Transformational Philanthropy: An Exploration* (2010) Retrieved from https://duaneelgin.com/wp-content/uploads/2010/11/transformational_philanthropy.pdf

Emmons, D. R. (2007). *Thanks! How Practicing Gratitude Can Make You Happier*. Boston: Houghton Mifflin.

Engebreth, B. (n.d.). *Department of Numbers*. Retrieved from http://www.deptofnumbers.com/income/us/

Fondo Centroamericano de Mujeres. (n.d.). Retrieved from https://www.fcmujeres.org/en/filantropia-feminista/

Foundation Center. (n.d.). Retrieved from http://foundationcenter.org/

Francis, P. (n.d.). *LAUDATO SI'*. Retrieved from http://w2.vatican.va/content/francesco/en/encyclicals/documents/papa-francesco_20150524_enciclica-laudato-si.html.

Frank, R. (2012, August 20). *CNBC.com*. Retrieved from http://www.cnbc.com/id/48725147

Frankl, V. (2006). *Man's Search for Meaning*. Boston: Beacon Press.

Friedman, T. L. (2016). *Thank You For Being Late: An Optimist's Guide to Thriving in the Age of Accelerations*. New York: Farrar, Straus and Giroux.

Froh, J. J., Emmons, R. A., Card, N. A., Bono, G., & Wilson, J. A. (2011). Gratitude and the Reduced Cost of Materialism in Adolescents. *Journal of Happiness Studies, 12, no. 2*, 300.

Fuller, B. (2015) Quote retrieved from https://www.bfi.org/ideaindex/projects/2015/community-architects-network

Gary, T. (2008). *Inspired Philanthropy*. San Francisco: Jossey-Bass.

Gawande, A. (2014). *Being Mortal: Medicine and What Matters in the End*. New York: Henry Holt & Company.

Gill, C., & Wagner, C. (n.d.). Retrieved from Philanthropy Women: https://philanthropywomen.org/womens-funds/feminist-philanthropy-relationship-reasons/

Gilovich, T. (2014, September). *Greater Good*. Retrieved from http://greatergood.berkeley.edu/gg_live/greater_good_gratitude_summit/speaker/thomas_gilovich/cultivating_gratitude_in_a_consumerist_society/?utm_source=GGSC+Newsletter+%232+-+September+2014&utm_campaign=GG+Newsletter+%232+-+September+2014&utm_medium=emai

Green Belt Movement. (n.d.). Retrieved from http://www.greenbeltmovement.org/

Harford, T. (2015, January 20). *Tim Harford The Undercover Economist*. Retrieved from http://timharford.com/2015/01/the-power-of-saying-no/

Hawken, P. (2017). *Drawdown: The Most Comprehensive*

Plan Ever Proposed to Reverse Global Warming. New York: Penguin Books.

Huffington, A. (2015). *Thrive*. New York: Harmony.

Illingworth, P., Pogge, T., Wenar, L. (2011) *Giving Well: The Ethics of Philanthropy*. Retrieved from https://www.oxfordscholarship.com/view/10.1093/acprof:oso/9780199739073.001.0001/acprof-9780199739073

Kayoussi, B. (2012, August 21). *Huffington Post*. Retrieved from http://www.huffingtonpost.com/2012/08/21/rich-people-charitable-giving_n_1819142.html

Killingsworth, M. (n.d.). Track Your Happiness. https://www.trackyourhappiness.org/. http://ed.ted.com/lessons/want-to-be-happier-stay-in-the-moment-matt-killingsworth. Retrieved from https://www.trackyourhappiness.org/

Le, P. (2015, June 30). *The Seattle Times*. Retrieved from http://www.seattletimes.com/seattle-news/girl-scouts-refuse-100000-anti-transgender-donation/

Leonard, A. (2009) Retrieved from Bioneers. https://bioneers.org/annie-leonard-the-story-of-stuff-bioneers/

Levins, N. (2013, December 26). *Urban Institute*. Retrieved from Urban Wire: https://www.urban.org/urban-wire/six-fast-facts-about-charitable-giving

Luhby, T. (2018, May 18). *Money*. Retrieved from www.money.cnn.com: http://money.cnn.com/2018/05/17/news/economy/us-middle-class-basics-study/index.html

Marek, K. (2014). *Stronger Together: What a Pioneering Feminist Philanthropist Is Thinking About Now*. Retrieved from Inside Philanthropy: https://www.insidephilanthropy.com/home/2016/9/20/stronger-together-what-a-pioneering-feminist-philanthropist.html

McCullough, M. E., & Emmons, R. A. (2003). Counting Blessings Versus Burdens: An Experimental Investigation of

Gratitude and Subjective Well-Being in Daily Life. *Journal of Personality and Social Psychology, 84 (2)*, 377-389.

McKibben, B. (2008). *Deep Economy*. St. Martin's Griffin.

Melton, G. D. (n.d.). *Together Rising*. Retrieved from http://togetherrising.org/about/

Morgan, G., & Ramírez, R. (1984). *Action Learning: A Holographic Metaphor for Guiding Social Change*. Retrieved from https://journals.sagepub.com/doi/10.1177/001872678403700101

Nordhoff, N. quote (2006). Retrieved from https://www.bizjournals.com/seattle/stories/2006/03/27/newscolumn2.html

O'Brien, B. (2014, December 16). Retrieved from http://buddhism.about.com/od/theeightfoldpath/a/rightlivelihood.htm

Olivet, J., Dones, M., Richard, M., Wilkey, C., Yampolskaya, S., Beit-Arie, M., & Joseph, L. (2018, March). *http://center4si.com/*. Retrieved from The Center for Social Innovation: http://center4si.com/wp-content/uploads/2016/08/SPARC-Phase-1-Findings-March-2018.pdf

Ord, T. (n.d.). *Giving What We Can*. Retrieved from https://www.givingwhatwecan.org/

Pachamama Alliance. (n.d.). Retrieved from https://www.pachamama.org/

PBS. (2011). Retrieved from Adventures in Learning/Teaching Kids About Charity: https://www.youtube.com/watch?v=p29dKpHnPjQ

Peavey, F. (1995). *Strategic Questioning: An approach to creating personal and social change*. Retrieved from The Change Agency: http://www.thechangeagency.org/campaigners-toolkit/links/strategic-questioning/

Philanthropy New York. Retrieved from https://philanthropynewyork.org/sites/default/files/resources/History%20of%20Philanthropy.pdf

Reeves, R. V. (2017). *Dream Hoarders: How the American Upper Middle Class is Leaving Everyone Else in the Dust, Why That Is a Problem, and What to Do About It.* Washington, D.C.: Brookings Institution Press.

Robin, V., & Dominguez, J. (1992). *Your Money or Your Life.* New York: Penguin Books.

Rockefeller, M. (n.d.). Retrieved from www.flowfunding.org

Schumacher, E. (1973). *Small is Beautiful, Economics as if People Mattered.* London: Blond & Briggs Ltd.

Scott, B. (2014) Hector Montoya quote, retrieved from https://www.nbcdfw.com/news/local/Family-Gives-PS4-To-Generous-9-Year-Old-Boy-255955581.html

Senior, J. (2014). *All Joy and No Fun, The Paradox of Modern Parenthood.* Ecco Books.

Shah, A. (1998-2016). *Global Issues.* Retrieved from http://www.globalissues.org/article/26/poverty-facts-and-stats

Shriver, T. (2014). *"Ripples in the World: CAC Multipliers".* Retrieved from www.cac.org: http://bit.ly/2zIv94S

Stan, A. M. (2013, November 20). Retrieved from Rewire: https://rewire.news/article/2013/11/20/if-we-each-have-a-torch-theres-a-lot-more-light-gloria-steinem-accepts-the-presidential-medal-of-freedom/

Steindl-Rast, D. (1984). *Gratefulness, The Heart of Prayer: An Approach to Life in Fullness.* New Jersey: Paulist Press.

The Girl Effect. (n.d.). Retrieved from girleffect.org: http://www.girleffect.org/why-girls/

Tierney, T. J., & Fleishman, J. L. (2011). *Give Smart, Philanthropy That Gets Results* Thomas J. Tierney. New York: PublicAffairs.

Tutu, D. (2015) Retrieved from http://www.tutufoundationusa.

org/2015/10/07/10-pieces-of-wisdom-from-desmond-tutu-on-his-birthday/

Twist, L. (2003). *The Soul of Money*. New York: W.W. Norton & Company.

Waldinger, R. (2015, November). *TED*. Retrieved from TEDxBakerStreet: http://www.ted.com/talks/robert_waldinger_what_makes_a_good_life_lessons_from_the_longest_study_on_happiness

Walker, D. (2015, December 17). *New York Times*. Retrieved from www.newyorktimes.com: https://mobile.nytimes.com/2015/12/18/opinion/why-giving-back-isnt-enough.html?_r=0&referer=http://mail01.tinyletterapp.com/brian-walsh/all-things-impact-a-21st-century-gospel-of-wealth-improved-regulatory-framework-for-impact-investing-just-capital-and-pi

Wheatley, M. (2006) *Leadership and the New Science: Discovering Order in a Chaotic World*.

Wiederkehr, M. (2010). *Seven Sacred Pauses*. Notre Dame: Sorin Books.

Wihbey, J. (2013, July 11). *Journalist's Resource*. Retrieved from http://journalistsresource.org/studies/society/social-media/multitasking-social-media-distraction-what-does-research-say

Woolley-Barker, T. (2016, March 25). *Medium*. Retrieved from https://medium.com/@BiomimicryInst: https://medium.com/@BiomimicryInst/want-to-build-an-organization-that-lasts-create-a-superorganism-3e4318b172d#.gdze2arqc

The Author

Kristen Corning Bedford is an author, speaker and philanthropic strategist. Through her writing and consulting, Kristen helps individuals, businesses, and foundations create sustainable and strategic giving plans that align privilege with purpose.

Kristen is a thought partner and facilitator who is passionate about bringing people together to create change. She is the cofounder of The Ruby Room, for which she received the Northwest Girls Coalition's Outstanding Community Leadership Award. She served as the president of the Board of Directors of ArtsEd Washington, and was a founding board member of Urban Homestead Foundation. She is a founding member of the investment club Women Investing in Tacoma and the giving circle Impact | West Seattle. She was nominated for Antioch University's Horace Mann Award, and recognized as a South Sound 40 under 40 Leader. In her position as vice president of Community Philanthropy at The Greater Tacoma Community Foundation, she had the pleasure of developing and managing the Youth Against Violence Initiative, which resulted in the formation of a Youth Philanthropy Board and earned the Foundation a Leadership Legacy Award from the Center for Ethical Leadership. Kristen is currently on the Board of the Whidbey Institute and a member of the Family Committee for Equity and Inclusion at Genesee Hill Elementary.

Kristen received her MA from Antioch University in Whole Systems Design and her BA from Western Washington University in Film Studies and Production. She is a Seattle native currently living in West Seattle with her husband and two young sons, who keep her ever mindful of legacy and generosity.

A Generous Heart
Changing the World Through Feminist Philanthropy
Copyright © Kristen Corning Bedford 2019

ISBN 978-1692565282

All Rights Reserved

Cover Design by Kerry Hynds
Interior Design by Mary Holste